Reflections of a Servant Leader

My Journey as the Longest Serving Airman in U.S. Air Force History

Major General, Retired
Alfred K. Flowers

TABLE OF CONTENTS

ACKNOWLEDGEMENTS

I WOULD LIKE TO THANK my family, the many leaders, co-workers and peers for their support and inspiration over many years. The experiences from interacting and serving with all of you inspired me in this endeavor.

I owe a great debt of gratitude to my spouse and son, Mrs. Ida and Colonel Al Flowers Jr., for their support over the years and continuing to give me a nudge when I got lazy with the idea of launching a book mission.

Special thanks to Major General, retired Joe Ward. Joe wrote the Foreword, was a strong motivator and always said "You have to tell the story in a book." He was relentless in following up frequently just to see how things were proceeding. I am forever grateful for friends like Joe.

Finally, I want to thank Kevin Quirk, for his assistance with the writing, mentorship and support. This book would be far from finished if it were not for Kevin's support.

Foreword

I FIRST MET GENERAL FLOWERS more than twenty-five years ago. The year was 1990. He was serving as a Major in the United States Air Force and I was a young Captain. I did not know then how blessed I was to have met the then Major Al Flowers and how prominent a role he would play in the annals of United States Air Force leadership in the years to come. The Air Force history books, at that point in time, had not yet captured the Airman who served the longest, an amazing forty-six years in uniform—a record impossible for anyone to top.

Fast forward to the year 2012, on the momentous occasion of General Flowers' retirement from active duty when the impact of this extraordinary Airman was brought into full focus. General Flowers' Air Force canvas painting was complete and it's a magnificent masterpiece.

Alfred K. Flowers came from very humble beginnings and looked to the military to improve his socio-economic standing. At age seventeen, he enlisted in the Air Force. He quickly hit his stride wearing our nation's cloth. Promotions added stripes to his sleeves and confidence in his ability to lead Airmen. Airman Flowers was ready to expand and multiply his impact in the Air Force through a transition from the enlisted corps to becoming an officer. It wasn't going to be easy. He encountered turbulence and rejection, but he persevered. Twice he applied to Officer Training School (OTS) and was turned down. He applied a third time and was finally granted an opportunity to join the Officer Corps.

His selection to OTS had far-reaching benefits, as he quickly ascended the officer ranks while simultaneously increasing his sphere of influence. He mentored legions of Airmen, encouraging them to follow his True North of integrity first! His positive impact on the world's greatest Air Force continues to yield incredible results as his General Officer tree grows new branches and bears new fruit.

No other officer has had a more significant impact on my military career, and I am forever grateful to General Flowers for that. To reminisce, as the years passed by after our first meeting our career paths often intertwined. With each connection and interaction came the unveiling of an amazing story, one I am very glad is about to be told. On two separate occasions, General Flowers was my direct supervisor at the Pentagon. The day-to-day engagements that ensued during those Pentagon tours provided me with a close-up look at one of our nation's finest leaders and the values he emphasized that served as the underpinning for his extraordinary success.

I loved his leadership style. He absolutely refused to take credit for anything that went well on his watch; indeed, he always passed on credit and praise to his troops. Whenever his team encountered difficulties, he stood up to *take the heat*, never putting any blame on his subordinates. He always *had our back*. As a result, he earned the loyalty, respect and admiration of all who were privileged to serve with him. He knew how positivity motivates his team and he understood how to help his fellow Airmen reach their God-given potential. He always maintained that true success is not measured by the number of medals on your chest or the number of stars on your shoulder but by your impact on others. In the end, it is the legacy we leave behind that ultimately determines and defines our value as a leader.

I remember the day I was selected to the flag and General Officer ranks. After I delivered the fantastic news to my wife and parents, I called Brigadier General Flowers to ask him to officiate my pin-on ceremony. There was no one else I wanted next to me on stage than the one I revered and the one who had served as my role model for so many years. At that time, General Flowers was getting ready to pin on his second star, so I requested a special favor. I asked him if I could wear his one-star rank as he got ready to pin on Major General. He was quiet on the other end of the phone, not responding with a simple "yes" or "no." I awkwardly switched subjects and we soon ended the conversation.

A few months later, the day had arrived for my promotion ceremony. I had purchased my new one-star rank and was anxious to have General Flowers pin them on my shoulders. A young Airman who was assisting with the ceremony had the newly purchased stars on a blue pillow ready to pass to General Flowers, but he waved off the young Airman. "Joe, do you remember your special request?" he asked. I said, "Yes, sir, I do." He then reached into his pocket and pulled out the one-star rank he had worn as a Brigadier General. He said he would be proud to have me wear them. I was elated beyond measure that he had remembered my special request! It should not have surprised me when he delivered. Throughout his many years of service he answered a myriad of "special requests." He would end each evening in private thought, seeking opportunities to help his fellow Airmen, to make a positive difference in the lives of subordinates. By every conceivable measure, he is the consummate servant leader.

I firmly believe servant leadership is the highest calling of the many leadership styles. It is a manifestation born from within the heart and serves as the guiding light for great leaders. One's heart populates the fertile field from which servant leadership is harvested, season after season. Al Flowers is a General who leads from the heart. In fact, his heart is much larger than the stars he wore on his shoulder. He would not let rank or ego interfere with his desired aim: simply to help others and to serve with honor. In every decision he made, he always thought first of the impact his decision would have on the enlisted force. Serving for thirteen years in the enlisted ranks gave him a sturdy grounding and deep understanding of the significant role our enlisted men and women play in our nation's defense. The General will tell you the enlisted force is the backbone and pulse of our Armed Forces.

The story of General Al Flowers will serve as a true inspiration to many. It will affirm that the American Dream is still very much alive and within the grasp of every American, regardless of race, ethnicity or any other discriminator. General Flowers' winning formula of faith, hard work and dedication to helping others is a matter of personal choice. It offers anyone who ascribes to his secrets to success the same rocket fuel that enabled General Flowers to rise from picking tobacco leaves at a "princely" sum of fifty cents an hour in rural North Carolina to earning a place in the pantheon of our nation's greatest Air Force Generals.

Finally, at a time when our nation needs a strong dose of inspirational servant leadership, this book answers the call. It provides the magic elixir needed to generate a spark. It is an encouragement to all, whether you are serving in uniform or in corporate America. General Flowers' timeless wisdom and sage advice has helped scores of officers and civilians and will help you. Everyone can benefit from this remarkable story.

This book provides a unique opportunity to get to know the man behind the record: the longest serving Airman in the history of the United States Air Force and the longest serving African American in the Department of Defense. What was his recipe for success? What motivated him to spend nearly a half century on active duty in the Armed Forces? How can we benefit from his unsurpassed example of service-before-self? The answers to these and many other key questions are about to unfold. So buckle in; this promises to be an incredible ride from the tobacco fields of North Carolina to the jungles of Vietnam to the highest echelons within the Department of Defense. Enjoy the read, and Aim High!

Major General Joseph S. Ward Jr.
United States Air Force (Retired)
One Nation Under God

INTRODUCTION

I NEVER DREAMED of becoming a history-maker. Growing up in a family of sharecroppers in rural eastern North Carolina in the 1950s and early '60s, I did not hold any grandiose ambitions. I just wanted to find a way out. Living day to day amid economic, social and educational hardship in the segregated South, I only imagined that there had to be something better, something more. I didn't know what it was or how I was going to get there, but I was determined and passionate about discovering a new path and following it to the best of my ability.

That path led me to enlist in the United States Air Force as a seventeen year old and to devote my entire adult career to serving our country. When I retired on January 1, 2012 after forty-six years, five months and twenty-four days of active service, I was noted as being the longest serving airman in the history of the Air Force. I was also recognized as the longest-serving active-duty African American in all the branches in the history of the Defense Department. I had achieved the rank of Major General and, in my last assignment as Deputy Assistant Secretary for Budget, Office of the Assistant Secretary of the Air Force, I was entrusted with managing the entire $170 billion annual Air Force budget.

No, I could never have foreseen such achievements and success when I was growing up. Looking back, I would have to say that joining the Air Force was the best decision I ever made. I came in because I had to, I stayed because I wanted to, and if I had to do it all over again I would do it the same way. I can also say that whatever I accomplished or achieved, it was not about *me*; it was always about *we*. As I often tell my colleagues and friends, I'm just "Airman Ordinary." Yes, I worked hard, played fair and tried to rise above my situation and better myself. However, I truly owe my success to the people who served with me. It was their dedication, their abilities, their commitment to excellence, their willingness to do whatever needed to be done at every step of the way that enabled me to get where I was able to go. None of us who are leaders are smart enough or talented enough to do it alone.

When people ask me about how I view my legacy, I always smile. I explain that my legacy is not what I take with me, or what I have achieved personally. My legacy is what I leave behind. To put that in the more colorful language that I call upon in my motivational talks to groups and organizations these days, legacy is not what they put in the ground but who and what attends the funeral. My hope is that in all the assignments and responsibilities entrusted to me, I have made a difference. I always believed that if I somehow touched the lives of men and women who were doing excellent jobs, performing to the best of their ability, achieving greater success than they may have believed possible, then I would have indeed succeeded.

As a leader, trainer, mentor and guide, I can honestly say that I loved every day of my work. At night I would go to bed thinking about how I could make a difference the next day. I would imagine the specific challenges that would be presented that would provide opportunities to do something positive not only for the Air Force but for one airman's life. I really don't know how many lives I may have impacted, but I do know that every one of them were important. Those devoted servants are performing at a level equal to or greater than I did, and all of them are making vital contributions as American citizens.

It's been more than a few years now since my formal retirement ceremony held at Joint Base Anacostia-Bolling in Washington, but I remember that day vividly. The event was officiated by Secretary of the Air Force Michael B. Donley, a former boss of mine who quipped that "General Flowers served under nine Commanders in Chief...starting with General George Washington." Later in the ceremony I was deeply moved by a ritual of the passing of a folded American flag from one airman to another, each representing one of the ranks I had held during my service. While the flag was handed from one individual to the next, words were read to the poem *My Name Is Old Glory* by retired Air Force officer Don S. Miller. It ended with my own son, Air Force Colonel Alfred K. Flowers Jr., presenting the flag into my waiting arms for me to hold to my heart as hundreds of family members, close friends and colleagues looked on.

Since that memorable day, my mission has changed in some ways but it's not really different. I may not wear the uniform of a Major General every day anymore, but I am still committed to making a difference in the lives of those around me. When I address military or civilian individuals and groups, I tell my story and share what I have learned on my own journey in the hope that it may reach, encourage or inspire those who are seeking guidance on their own path toward success and fulfillment. Now I am grateful for this opportunity to extend this message to *you*.

I don't know exactly why you may have picked up this book.

Perhaps, like me many decades ago, you are a young (or not so young) person struggling with economic, social or educational challenges. You may feel stuck or discouraged, wondering how you can ever get out of your situation. Perhaps you have been knocked down by some recent setback, whether financial, physical or emotional, and you're looking for something that will help provide the lift you need to get up off the ground, begin to rebuild, and set your sights on improving your life. Maybe you are considering entering the military and seek guidance on what to expect and how to navigate the terrain. Then again, you may be someone who has already achieved a degree of success, rising above your own hardships or challenges, but you sense that there is something more available to you and you're not sure how and where to find it. If you are a leader seeking to grow and evolve, you may be hungry for new ideas, insights and hands-on examples to assist you in soaring toward greater heights.

Whether you have arrived here for any of these reasons, or because of something totally different, I welcome you. It doesn't matter if you are a man or a woman. It doesn't matter how old you are, where you live, or what your personal beliefs may be. It only matters that you're open and receptive to listen and to learn. As you read on, I trust that you will discover something that will be of value to you in pushing through whatever roadblocks may be in your way. Always remember that you are important and that success in any realm of life is absolutely possible for you, if you have the right attitude and embrace the critical foundations of success. If in some way I can play a part in reminding you of that, and providing you the guidance and the inspiration that will enable you to find a way out of any difficult situation you may be in and unlock the door to what you can achieve, I will be grateful for the opportunity.

I don't have all the answers for you. Only *you* have those answers. Only you can do the work to get where you want to go. But none of us are alone as we strive for what we want and what will truly fulfill us. As you summon the wisdom and the capacity to tap your full potential, I will be proud to serve as your ally.

I know that some of you may have already joined the Air Force or one of the other military services, or you are considering moving in that direction. If so, thank you for your service or your sincere interest in serving our country! Because so many of my own experiences evolved during my time in the Air Force, I trust that you will relate to what I share. You will also find in these pages specific tools and advice for launching and navigating a successful military career.

If you are working in the civilian world, or you haven't yet set your sails toward one specific direction in work or career, I believe that you too will resonate with much of what I have to say. I wasn't born in a uniform and when I die the people who bury me won't be wearing one either. We are all just regular people trying our best to find meaning and purpose, to embrace healthy values, and to live the right way.

After I walk you through my personal story, I will introduce many of the simple but valuable messages that I offer to audiences whenever I speak. I will spell out, literally, some of the key components of success and fulfillment in a way that will be easy for you to grasp. I also will outline some of the key attributes and attitudes of effective leadership, whether inside or outside of the military.

Looking beyond our individual efforts to overcome personal challenges, I also will point toward what any of us who are committed to helping others can do as a community today. We can all make a difference in the lives of men and women who urgently need guidance, encouragement and support. Let's come together to offer our wisdom and our gifts. This world really can be a better place, and no matter our race, religion or political persuasion, we all have the opportunity to help make that happen.

So let's get started. Allow me to begin by escorting you back to the days when the term "sharecropper" was not something people read about in a history book. It was real and I was living it. Hang on tight and I'll take you on a ride to witness this very different time and place.

A FAMILY OF SHARECROPPERS

I WAS TEN YEARS OLD when my grandmother told me the story of my arrival into this world. On December 29, 1947, I was born premature, weighing in at no more than three pounds. The hospital available to African Americans in rural Jones County in eastern North Carolina at that time lacked the facilities to properly care for premature babies, and my grandparents who had generously agreed to raise me lacked any kind of bassinet. So they had to improvise. They brought me home in a shoebox.

Apparently the winter of '48 was a cold and harsh one, which meant heavy usage of the only source of heat in our four-room home: an old metal wood-burning heater that sat in the middle of the living room floor.

"Your grandfather and your uncle would go out in the woods around here and cut wood and bring it in," my grandmother explained to me. "They always made sure there was enough wood to keep that heater burning all night long. I would sit you right by that heater with me through the night to keep you warm. You were so small."

That heater was my incubator, and my grandmother kept me alive. As I approach my seventieth birthday, there is not a day that goes by that I am not filled with appreciation and gratitude for how my grandmother, Lucy Rhodes Roberts, nourished and sustained me through that first long winter and throughout my childhood in a family of sharecroppers.

I called my grandmother "Mama" and my grandfather "Daddy" because to me they were always my parents. My mother and father were teenagers when I was conceived, and my father left soon after I was born. They decided that they were not prepared to raise a child when in many ways they were still children themselves. "I did the best I could at the time," my mother would say to me as the years went by. She remained living in the area, remarried and raised a son. My father had eleven children, eight girls and three boys, after my birth. Once in a great while he stopped by and handed me a couple of dollars, but around my family circle in early life I was the "other child." My grandparents weren't much for talking about it either. "Your father left you and married another woman and had more children, but that's someone you just don't need to concern yourself with now," Mama would say to me when the subject came up.

I am not angry or bitter about the choices that my parents made concerning my upbringing. In many ways, I had the best "parents" anyone could ever ask for. My grandparents graciously accepted the task of raising me because their own daughter had a child as a teenager and wasn't able to take care of him. They felt a responsibility to step in. And in steering me toward adulthood, they provided me the love and support that enabled me to persevere through every hardship we encountered.

Life for a family of sharecroppers during the 1950s and early '60s meant hard physical labor, limited opportunities and a system that somehow or other always seemed to hold us down with little or no real income or resources to lift ourselves up. We did at least have a home to live in, although it was owned by our landlord. It was a tiny house, probably no more than 700 or 800 square feet. With no bathroom, we had to rely on an outhouse located out back, by the pack house where we stored and prepared the corn and tobacco that we grew and the stables where our old gray mules Mabel and Macy were housed. This outhouse was a simple wooden shed with a hole dug in the ground, and during those many years when we could not afford to buy toilet paper we would always make sure to bring an ample supply of newspapers or magazines with us when we headed out to cleanse ourselves. The house had a tin roof with holes in it. I recall many a night lying in my bed looking right up through those holes. As I swatted away the mosquitoes that kept biting me and gazed up at the sky and the stars, I would say to myself, "Everybody can't be living like this. There's got to be something better out there."

In return for our primitive housing, we tended our landlord's farm, primarily raising tobacco and corn. Our landlord earned the first fifty percent of any income earned from our labor, and my grandfather was supposed to receive the other fifty percent. The only problem with that arrangement was that we were charged for our farming supplies and all the food and incidentals we bought at the landlord's store, and once all those fees were deducted after the harvest every year, my grandfather would usually turn to my grandmother and report, "Well, Lucy, looks like we still owe the landlord $300."

My mother had been raised in the same sharecropper household, and my father's parents had been sharecroppers as well, all in the same tiny community of Phillips Crossroads. Our landlord owned much of the land in the town. Another landlord family in our town owned the land that my Aunt Ethel and Uncle William and other relatives lived and worked on.

Our sharecropper family spread far and wide within the community. We even had extended family members sharing our small house on the corner of a little dirt road and a narrow paved street. My mother's brother Walter lived with us, as he was my grandparents' son. We called him Buddy. Although he was biologically my uncle, I thought of Buddy as my brother. He was sixteen years older than me and we shared the same bedroom. The other family member crammed into our home was my great-grandmother Marzella Roberts, whom I called Grandmama or Miss Marzella. With just two bedrooms, a living room and a kitchen, there weren't many options for where my great-grandmother would sleep. So for most of my childhood and adolescence she lived with my grandparents in their bedroom. From everything that I could observe, everyone got along just fine. It's amazing when you think about it—what wife today would agree to share her and her husband's bedroom with her mother-in-law? Back then, we all had learned to make the best of the hand that was dealt to us, and we understood that our day-to-day survival relied on a strong foundation of mutual acceptance and respect.

I have fond memories of Grandmama. I remember when she would turn to me and say, "Boy, go get me a snuff brush." I knew exactly what that meant. I was to go out and pull down a limb about the size of a pen from one of the old trees in our yard, and then bring it back to her. Then I would watch her chew the end of that limb until it got frayed and make a brush out of it. Next she would dip her favorite snuff onto the brush and put it in her mouth. She dipped that snuff every day. When she wasn't dipping snuff I might find her taking a shot of homemade corn whiskey from the little bottle she kept by her bed. As I grew up, I also came to appreciate how this simple and un-educated woman was very wise. She had strong, healthy values and a sharp understanding of how children should act. I believe she had a very positive influence on my grandmother in that regard, and my grandmother passed along those values to me.

My grandmother's mother, Isabella Rhodes, lived only about a mile away. I saw this great-grandmother often as well. My other grandmother, Erma Roberts, lived on Pine Street, also just a short walk from our home. She loved to fish, and sometimes I'd sit with her holding our cane fishing poles by the little creek on either side of the bridge on the main road. On a good day we might catch a few perch or catfish to eat. If we caught eels, we would throw them back. When you add in all the aunts, uncles and cousins nearby, we had a very strong sense of family.

We may never have had much money, but we did not go hungry. Our kitchen was small, with no room to move around the aluminum table and six chairs, but it was always a busy place. Not only did Mama prepare all our meals there, but the wood-fueled iron stove that she used for cooking was also utilized to heat water for our baths. The water was heated in a reservoir on the side of the stove.

We raised chickens and hogs for meat. Our landlord owned the pens where the hogs were kept, but at least we didn't have to share the meat with him. Every December or January we would slaughter five or six hogs and then proceed to salt the meat and hang it for smoking. For months we would feast on roast pork, fried pork, hams, shoulders, bacon and sausage. Mama would prepare the meat with lard, which was produced by frying off the fat from the meat. We didn't know it at the time, and probably couldn't have done anything about it anyway, but cooking and eating that way was a surefire recipe for hypertension. Both my grandparents had high blood pressure, and so did my mother and many others in our family. I've been on high blood pressure medication for several years myself. That was simply one more price we had to pay for having a place to live and food to eat.

The chickens were a vital source of eggs, and the eggs that we didn't eat ourselves we would sometimes barter for fish from the old man who would come by in his fish truck once or twice a week. We were partial to spots, which I still consider an eastern North Carolina specialty, as well as mullets and Atlantic croakers, a silvery pink fish that made a distinctive croaking sound when cooked. We'd also eat our chickens when it was time. With an ample supply of corn in the pack house, Mama would set some aside to make cornmeal, which yielded delicious bread. Our garden produced an ample supply of potatoes, beans, carrots, beets and other vegetables. To this day, I still love beets and I savor a dish of Irish potatoes and string beans, something Mama loved to make.

I always knew what we would have for breakfast on Sunday mornings before church: fried chicken, biscuits and peaches packed in a can with syrup. Back then, you could not have told me that this was anything less than a gourmet delight! The funny thing is, we really did have a gourmet treat from time to time without even realizing it. Every spring my grandfather, Buddy and I would go out "shadding," which was basically fishing with a net for shad. We especially enjoyed eating the eggs from the female shad, which we called "roes" or roses. Little did we know that we were partaking in the delicacy of caviar!

When I was about ten years old, Mama and Daddy ushered me through an important passage point. Long about the time that my grandmother informed me of how my grandfather and uncle would cut the wood to fuel the stove that kept me warm and safe when I was an infant, I was invited to go out on those wood-chopping runs with them. In addition to cutting down wood for our heating and cooking, we would also hunt rabbits and squirrels. I took pride in making the rabbit boxes and putting carrots in them to catch the rabbits.

"Kendell, look at how you can help now," Mama pointed out. Everyone in my family called me by my middle name, Kendell, which many in North Carolina still call me today. "You're out there with your granddaddy helping to cut that wood, and you're catching rabbits and squirrels to help feed us all. Instead of having others do things for you to keep you warm and safe, you are keeping yourself warm. Think about how far you have come."

That lesson stuck with me throughout my career in the Air Force, both as it applied to me as well as to others whom I guided or mentored. It's important to make note of those times when you are able to do something that you could not have done earlier. Give yourself credit and use that understanding to move on to the next task or assignment to master.

I began school when I was five years old. The schools available to families like ours were not only segregated, they were what you might call primitive. The Phillips Crossroads School was just an old two-room house in the country, about a mile from our home. One room was for first and second grade, the other room for third and fourth grade. The instruction was pretty basic: the teacher gave you the books for your grade and you were told to work with them on your own, going as fast or as slow as you needed to. Since I did okay with the first-grade books, it wasn't long before I was given the second-grade books. I walked to school with my older cousin Alvania and at lunch I would sit outside that schoolhouse under an old oak tree and eat what my grandmother had sent along with me, usually a molasses biscuit. On a good day I might have a ham biscuit and on a really good day I might have five cents to buy a cup of milk.

I remember one teacher from that school, Ms. Kornegay, because she showed a sincere interest in me as a student and as a person. I believe that she wanted all of us who were economically, socially and environmentally deprived to reach for a better life. She encouraged my love of arithmetic and mathematics, and when I got into trouble at school she somehow made sure that Mama and Daddy knew about it...even before I got home. The party line that still functioned in our phone system was buzzing.

"Well, the teacher said that you had a little problem today," Mama would say as I walked in the door. My offense would usually be something like making little paper airplanes and flying them around the schoolroom. Or maybe I would fold a piece of paper to make "poppers," so named because of the noise they made when you snapped them. When I think back to my teacher making sure that my parents knew when I had caused that little bit of mischief, I am reminded of one of the major benefits of growing up at that time in that environment: we were raised not just by our parents but by the whole village. Everyone in our community cared about one another and looked out for each other. That's how we survived.

By fifth grade I had moved on to Trenton Elementary School. Trenton was the closest "real" town to us, and although the school was still segregated at least we had more formal instruction. I completed grades five through eight there before moving on to Jones High School.

Every year before school started, my grandparents would take me shopping for school clothes: a couple of pairs of jeans, two or three shirts and one pair of brogan shoes. That was it for school clothes for the year. As a typical schoolboy back then, I would spend a lot of time down on my knees shooting marbles or playing other kids' games. After two or three months those jeans would begin to turn gray, and halfway through the school year the holes would begin to show. Mama would simply iron on those blue jean patches that were popular back then. In winter, when the rain and cold would make the toes of my brogans turn up and get hard, Daddy would take out some motor oil, rub it on my shoes and sit them by the old wooden heater overnight to soften them up. The next morning I would put those same shoes back on and just keep on going. Occasionally during the school year, I would wear holes in the soles and would have to insert some cardboard.

My daily responsibilities did not end with going to school and doing my homework. Daddy needed all the help that he could get, and he had me working on the farm by the time I was ten. In the 1950s and early '60s in North Carolina, tobacco ruled. So it was natural that tobacco, as well as corn, were the mainstays of our farming.

Growing tobacco was an almost year-round process. We would plant the tobacco seeds in late winter or early spring. You actually planted them in a bed and covered them with plastic until they began to germinate. Once that happened, you would take the plastic off and put a cloth over them, making a web, until they got large enough for you to open them up to the elements and let them grow. By April or May, after the last frosts, we would pull those plants that we planted in beds and set them out in the fields, just as you might set out flowers. That's when the tobacco really started to grow.

Later in the spring, we planted the corn. Work was always physically demanding because we did not have the benefit of the most modern farming equipment of that time period. During the cultivation period, we would be out there every day with our plow and our old gray mules Macy and Mabel. We did all the weeding by hand with hoes.

When harvest season approached, we moved toward the process of cropping tobacco, which is simply referred to today as picking tobacco. You would walk between the rows of tobacco, bend over and pull off the tobacco leaves. As you plucked out the tobacco leaves, you would tuck them under your arms until you get an armful, and then you would put the tobacco in the wooden trucks pulled by the mules. When the truck was filled, you'd take it to the barn where other folks would put the tobacco on a stick. They called that "looping tobacco." They would loop the tobacco, put it on a stick, and hang it up in the barn. Our barn was small but it was large enough to fit in rafters, which were poles that ran across the barn for us to hang the sticks on. The rafters would be five tiers high, about three feet apart. As soon as my legs got long enough to straddle those poles, I would stand up there and take the sticks others handed to me and then hang them. Then I would go up one more tier and hang more sticks, and up again one more tier to hang more sticks. They called that "hanging tobacco."

Once we got the barn full of hanging tobacco, we would light the oil burners to begin the process of curing the tobacco. We had six or seven oil burners, but in the first week you would light only one or two of them every day. This began the two-week drying process. You would gradually increase the heat, knowing that if you made it too hot right away it would ruin the tobacco. After about a week you could light all the burners, and the tobacco that had been green would turn brown or yellow. It cured at different colors based upon the quality of the leaves that were picked at the time.

When you first began to crop the tobacco, the tobacco leaves that you were pulling off the stalks were called "sand lugs." Each week or so, as the tobacco became riper, you would pick more. It would take about six weeks to pick it all.

Next we would take the cured tobacco to our pack house, take it off the sticks and sort it based on the grade of tobacco. Finally we would haul the tobacco to a warehouse in the nearby city of Kinston where auctioneers would come through and buy the tobacco at a price determined by its quality. Sometimes we would haul the tobacco forty miles away to a warehouse in Farmville, probably because Daddy thought he could get a better price there. From those warehouses the tobacco would be shipped off to the many tobacco processing plants in North Carolina to be turned into cigarettes, snuff or whatever they were going to produce from it. Back then, we didn't give one thought to the potential physical harm of smoking tobacco products. Tobacco growing was the number one industry of the state, and it was a vital part of what sustained us.

Once we got the tobacco harvested, it would be time to harvest the corn. Years later, farmers would be able to call upon mechanical pickers for corn, just as they did for tobacco. In our time, however, we had to do it all manually. When the corn would dry out and be ready to pick in late summer or early fall, we had to go out and break that corn off the stalks with our bare hands. We would gather the broken-off corn in piles, and when the piles got big enough we would throw the corn up into a wooden wagon pulled by Mabel and Macy. Then we would take the corn to the pack house to be stored until it was time to be sold, except for what we kept for ourselves.

Whether selling corn or tobacco, the same rules with our landlord applied. Our landlord would take his fifty percent off the top, but all of our bills, including what it cost us to produce the crops, would be taken out of our fifty percent share. It was a formula that somehow always seemed to work for their side, but not for ours. Still, at harvest time Daddy might have a few extra dollars to spend. When he did, he might stop by the fish market and buy five pounds of fish for a dollar and a half. Or, on very rare occasions, he might have enough money to purchase a little bit of beef, which Mama would roast for a very special meal. All the years while I was growing up, beef remained something mostly out of our family's reach.

Farm chores and school made for a very busy week, but on Sundays church became our family's focus. Most of our extended family attended services and Sunday school at Haughton Chapel Free Will Baptist Church near Trenton. My grandmother was a mother in the church and I eventually became a junior deacon while also singing in the junior choir. Church was an all-day commitment on Sundays. The service was at 11 o'clock and then, after a break for lunch, we would return for community gatherings and other church-related events in late afternoon and early evening. Sometimes Mama and Daddy would invite our pastor over to our home for Sunday lunch. Mama made her special cake, which she called sweet bread, to serve along with her best fried chicken. As a youngster, I have to admit that I didn't much look forward to those pastor visits. The preacher would always be served the best pieces of chicken, and I would be left eating the backs! Four times a year our church held a quarterly meeting, and for that important event a big meal would be served at church. They had to put chairs on the sides and in the aisles to accommodate the crowds. Church was another major part of the village that held us all together.

Sometimes on Saturdays I only had to work half the day on the farm. On those Saturdays, we often made the twenty-mile trek along Highway 58 to the "big" city of Kinston in Lenoir County. We would drive into the downtown area and walk along Queen Street, Kinston's main commercial street, just to see who was out walking and shopping. Sometimes I would stop in at one of the five-and-dimes, Roses or H.L. Green, where I would look forward to a fifteen-cent hot dog with chili and mustard.

The lunch counters were segregated, of course, and you wouldn't find any African Americans in many of the more upscale stores on nearby streets. At one of Kinston's most popular eateries located just outside of downtown, African Americans could not walk in the front door and eat in the main dining area. We were only allowed to pull up to the takeout window on the side of the building. When I was walking on Queen Street, I would have liked a milkshake at Standard Pharmacy, but that was beyond our budget. So were the movies at the Paramount Theatre. In all the years I lived in eastern North Carolina, I saw no more than four or five films. I didn't mind, though. Just being free to roam around downtown Kinston was a treat. Other kids from different backgrounds may have had more exciting outlets for fun, but I didn't know any better.

Another regular stop on those Saturday outings to town was at Grady's Café. They served hot dogs, but I would actually get to have a hamburger there sometimes. There was a good reason for that: my mother was the cook. When she was growing up, in the same sharecropper home that my grandparents raised me, my mother had yearned to find a way to get off the farm. Cooking was her ticket out. Although she advanced no further than ninth grade in school, she learned how to become an excellent cook and gained steady work at Grady's and other restaurants, including the one that was part of the Holiday Inn.

Long after divorcing my father, my mother also found herself living a much different lifestyle. She married my step-father, Augustus Miller, who was from a more affluent African American family and moved into a much nicer house. I would visit her there sometimes and spend time with my brother Uronus. Strictly speaking, he was my half-brother since we had the same mother and different fathers. But I've always looked at that distinction as irrelevant. As far as I was concerned, if someone was related to me because we had one parent in common, that person was my sister or brother, period.

Spending time at the home of my brother, my mother and my step-father came with some restrictions. I was most comfortable in the kitchen and one other room in my mother's house, as well as the porch and yard. The Millers lived in the Woodington area of Kinston, a different world from where my mother had been raised in Jones County. Two of my step-father's sisters actually graduated from college and became teachers. The family owned property and other resources, and my mother and step-father had a partnership in a funeral parlor in Kinston. To these folks, I was the child my mother had before she joined their family.

Still, my mother at least remained a part of my life. On Christmas, after we had a big meal of roast turkey and a ham, she might come over to our home and cook another meal, or we would spend part of Christmas at her home in Kinston. She and my step-father sometimes took me shopping in New Bern, a nicer city about forty-five minutes away, where they would buy me shirts, gloves or socks as Christmas gifts.

Day in and day out, however, I was in Jones County with my grandparents, living the life of a sharecropper. We celebrated Thanksgiving, Easter and other holidays with our own extended family. I don't remember birthdays as being special occasions, especially for me with my birthday just four days after Christmas. Whatever Mama and Daddy were able to afford for me, usually something simple and practical, they had already given me for Christmas. There would be no birthday presents or big birthday party.

Living a simple and mostly sheltered life, I got used to creating my own ways to enjoy myself when I had any time or opportunity to do so. I liked to play basketball and, since there was no way we would ever be able to afford a real basketball hoop and net, we had to improvise. Our basketball "hoop" was a bicycle rim that we'd nail to some scrap wood we used for a backboard. There was no net so we had to imagine that "swish" sound when you make a perfect shot. Inside, I decided that I would build my own gymnasium so I could play basketball when it was too wet or cold outside. I'd take a shoebox and nail it over the door of the bedroom that Buddy and I slept in. Then I would grab a sock and ball it up. All of a sudden I had a basketball and a hoop to shoot it through.

We had an old black-and-white TV, not that we had much time to watch it. Sometimes we would gather on Sunday evenings to catch *The Ed Sullivan Show,* and Daddy liked to watch the news or some football, baseball or wrestling now and then. The TV had an antenna out on the chimney. If we were getting a bad signal on one of the two or three stations we could pull in, my grandfather would direct me to go outside and turn the antenna until he would say, "Okay, it's better now."

At night I liked to listen to the radio show "Ernie's Record Parade" with host John R on WLAC in Nashville, Tennessee. The nationally popular program played blues and old songs, interspersed with ads for Ernie's Record Mart at 179 Third Avenue North in Nashville. WLAC had a powerful signal but I could not easily pick it up on our radio. Not to be denied, I went out to our driveway and sat in Daddy's 1951 Ford, which I was too young to drive. Many a night I would turn on the car radio and listen to my show, not realizing I was running the car battery down. When my "crime" was discovered, that was the end of that.

Every October I would eagerly anticipate the Jones County Fair with its Ferris wheel, carousel and all those enticing games. Our high school would dismiss the students at noon on Friday so we could all go to the fair. The game I could not resist was the one where you tossed the ring and tried to make it land over the top of a milk bottle. My strategy was to aim for the bottles close together in the middle. I figured that after the ring ricocheted around, it was certain to catch *one* of those bottles. So I would try and try, but I was never successful. That left me heartbroken not just because I had failed but because I had wasted a whole dollar trying to get a winner. You could buy three hot dogs and drinks at the five-and-dime in Kinston with that money, or you could purchase two packs of wieners at the store for fifty cents each. When we had some wieners, we would straighten out an old clothes hanger, put some dogs on it, and then stick the hanger over a corn cob fire. Oh yes, you learn to improvise when you're living in poverty.

Amidst all the hard work, the struggles and the limits of what was possible, it was always Mama that held us together. She was a wise woman, intelligent beyond her years of schooling. When she was thirteen years old and already doing her part on her family's farm, she became legally blind. I never heard the story of how it happened, but I do know that as a teenager she spent a great deal of time and energy educating herself by relating what she had been taught in school to what she was learning from others in her life. And then, somehow and some way, she regained her vision. She would often tell me how grateful she was to discover that she could see again. With no medical or professional treatment or intervention to point to, Mama had her own answer for what happened. It was her faith, her belief in God.

Faith was a vital part of what enabled me to persevere during my life in a family of sharecroppers, too. With the love and nurturance of my real parents, the foundation of a village where people actually cared for one another, and the hand of God, I made it through to the other side.

2

THE WISDOM OF
MODERN DAY SLAVERY

MAMA AND I WERE SITTING on the back porch one day peeling peaches that she was preparing to can. I noticed that she was throwing away the cores of her peaches, and without thinking about it much I just started gathering mine in a heap near my feet. As each new peach was peeled, I added the core to my growing pile.

"Kendell, what are you doing with those peach cores?" Mama asked finally.

"I'm saving them," I explained. "When we're finished, I am going to plant them so I can grow more peaches. Then I'm going to sell all those peaches and use the money to buy a house."

Mama didn't say a word. She just looked at me, silently nodded her head and went on with her peeling. It was an innocent dream for an eleven year old boy, but she understood how important it was to me. It was consistent with the same message that she had ingrained in me since I was five.

"I want you to go to school and get a good education," my grandmother would say. "I want you to do better than Daddy and I are able to do for you."

Looking back on my peaches plan now, I can see that I had already learned something essential about wanting and achieving success. I knew that if I really wanted a better life than the one we were living as a family of sharecroppers, it would not be something that someone just handed to me. I had to figure out how to create that better life myself.

So I did what my grandmother told me to do and focused on getting the best education I could gain from our segregated schools in Jones County. I was blessed with many supportive and encouraging teachers, as well as opportunities that did not come to every student in a poor rural area of the South during that time. In ninth grade at Jones High School in Trenton, my science teacher, Mr. Mills, nurtured my love of science and helped instill the confidence in me that I could achieve in the classroom and someday beyond it. That was a welcome buffer to the voices I often heard from some of my classmates, those who came from African American families who were less impoverished than us. Some of those families even owned property.

"You'll never leave the country. You'll never get off the farm," those other kids would tell me. "You'll just live here until you get old and your teeth start falling out. You don't have the background or the smarts to succeed."

Well, I may not have been intelligent about some things, but I certainly knew quite a bit about agriculture. Mr. Jordan, my agriculture teacher, recognized that. He selected me to be on a livestock judging team as part of the Future Farmers of America. Hogs and cattle were my specialty, and within the group of judges from the various schools in the area I was regarded as competent enough to serve as a judge at several of the top county fairs. That experience left an imprint on me, not only in terms of taking on greater responsibility but also in simply becoming an expert on livestock. Even today I will be traveling down some country road with my wife and I'll suddenly point out, "There's a Golden Guernsey" or "that one's a Jersey" or "over there are some Black Angus." She just shakes her head and laughs, "They'll never take the country out of you."

I also had natural ability in industrial arts, born from helping Daddy and Buddy make and fix things around the farm. I learned brick masonry in school and excelled at that. I also maintained my love for mathematics that had emerged in earlier grades. Ms. Nixon, my Business Math teacher, urged me to take my classes very seriously because my ability in this area could take me somewhere someday. That certainly proved to be excellent advice!

Around school and throughout our community, I was regarded as a responsible young man, someone who could be counted on to do the right thing. That perception opened the door to another opportunity. Not long after earning my driver's license I also acquired my bus driver's license. As difficult as it may be to imagine today, high school students were entrusted with driving the school busses that took students to and from the African American schools. The school principal and teachers got together to decide which students were mature enough for this assignment, and I was selected to be the driver of Bus Number 41, a forty-two-passenger bus that covered the immediate neighborhood where I lived. Many of my own relatives were among the forty-two students on my route.

Every morning I would leave home extra early, pick up all the students on my route, deliver them to school on time, park my bus and go off to class. When school was dismissed in the afternoon, I drove those same forty-two students home, brought the bus back to our house for the night, and proceeded to do my homework and go to work in the fields or the pack house.

The students all called me Kendell. I never once had an incident of serious misbehavior on the bus, even though many of my passengers were older than me, and I didn't have a single accident or citation on my record. There was something else I was proud of regarding my bus driver experience during my junior and senior year: I got paid $30 a month. That was big money for someone like me, and it paid for many a hamburger at the first Hardees that opened in Kinston in the early 1960s.

I can't say that I was a success at every attempt to excel or take on something new. I once tried to sing in a talent contest but lost the competition to a classmate whose family actually had a piano. Later, our high school guidance counselor selected me and five of my classmates to take a Navy ROTC test conducted in Raleigh. Since none of us had our own car, he loaned us his station wagon and appointed me as the driver for our group. We had a safe ride, but we didn't do so well in the test. I can still remember my confusion in trying to decipher a bunch of questions about maneuvers— where to bank left or right, or up or down. I had no clue what they were talking about. All six of us failed the test. As a side note, two of the group went on to earn PHDs, another is a retired attorney and still another is a school administrator. For a bunch of guys who royally flunked the Navy ROTC exam, I guess we didn't do too badly!

Taking on those added responsibilities like driving the school bus and judging livestock, as well as performing well as a student, all helped me to prepare for a life beyond sharecropping. However, during all the years of my childhood and much of my adolescence, I still had to maintain all my duties on our farm. It was my family's means of survival, and I was expected to do my part in the planting and harvesting of tobacco and corn and everything else we needed to do. I had to endure the back-breaking labor necessitated by doing the work without the benefit of modern equipment.

Those two old gray mules, Mabel and Macy, helped us when we cultivated our fields because we didn't have a tractor. We couldn't afford one, and our landlord did not provide us one. They did have their own tractor, and occasionally we were allowed to borrow it. Of course, they would always inspect the tractor carefully before allowing us to take it, with a promise to follow their strict rules, and then they'd inspect it again when we returned it. They explained that they just had to be careful because, you know, we might tear up their tractor.

So Mabel and Macy were always a central part of our lives, and a symbol for what we were living under. Sometimes I would vow that when I finally left home, by the time I got back Mabel and Macy would be gone. It was not that I disliked our animals. I just wanted the system of sharecropping as we had known it to be done away with. I didn't want anyone else to have to live under those same conditions.

Those rigid rules for borrowing a tractor represented just one more situation where we simply had to accept and abide by the terms of the sharecropper system. As I explained earlier, we bought most of our food on credit from the country store owned by our landlord. It was adjacent to their home and not far from ours. We also had to pay back the landlord for all the fertilizer, seeds and other farming supplies we needed to tend the fields. After harvest time, all those fees were taken out of our fifty percent share of what was earned, per the sharecropper agreement. The result was usually little or no profit—more likely a loss. For all that work that we did, we earned nothing in income, and when we were left with a debt after one year of farming, it would be carried over to the next year. So we would be faced with instantly borrowing more for our food and farming supplies and then had to hope for a bumper harvest that might push us out of debt and clear a few dollars' profit. That almost never seemed to happen.

The only way Daddy even knew that he finished a year in debt was that the landlord told him that he did. They never shared any of their accounting with him. The books were kept private. My grandfather tried to keep a paper record of what he owed, but he didn't have any way of knowing how much he was being charged for what our family borrowed and how much income had been earned from our labor. I'm not sure my grandfather was educated much beyond grade school, but he could add and subtract and he knew when he was being done right and when he was being done wrong. But even if he believed that something was not on the up and up with the figures kept by the landlord's family, he really didn't have much choice other than to accept it. In his perspective, if he chose to walk away from the farm because he was not being given what was justly his, he would become the head of a family of homeless people looking for someplace to live. That security of having a roof over our heads and enough food to eat trumped any sense of injustice about the sharecropper system. We had to survive, and for uneducated African Americans in rural North Carolina during that time, the options for finding a way to survive were minimal.

Daddy didn't talk about being treated unfairly by our landlord. I didn't really think too much about the injustices I had been living under myself until after I had moved on. When I consider it through the lens of today, after a career in finance in the Air Force, I believe that the attitude of landlords toward folks like our family working within the sharecropper system was pretty simple: you are subordinates, we are the landlord; take what we give you or go somewhere else. We were a source of making them money. Perhaps they assumed that people like my grandfather just weren't intelligent enough to recognize that they were being mistreated. They probably figured we were just poor, black people who would simply appreciate having a place to live and could be treated any way they wanted.

When I gathered my thoughts for writing this book, I began to see this picture in a further light. In recent years I had spent some time researching my family roots through ancestry.com and other resources. I discovered that the parents of my great-grandmother Isabella Rhodes and her husband Joseph Rhodes were slaves. That's not something that was mentioned around our home. Perhaps my grandparents were embarrassed about that part of their heritage. More likely they hid that information from us because they wanted our focus to be squarely on the future and building a better life, rather than dwelling on memories of where our ancestors had come from. But I would have liked to have known more about our family's roots in slavery. It's simply part of my history, and I'm not ashamed of it at all. I'm curious as to the conditions they lived under, how they were treated as slaves, the details surrounding their sale, the circumstances related to gaining their freedom and what they did with it, and what impact living in slavery had on them over the subsequent years. Unfortunately, when I tried to gather more clues about this important part of my heritage, I kept hitting dead ends. I did not have enough information to dig deeper.

However, simply uncovering the basic truth that my great-grandparents' parents were slaves left me thinking about the sharecropper system differently. I began chewing on this question: Were there any similarities to the life of a slave and the life of a family of sharecroppers like us?

I believe there were many similarities, starting with a basic injustice. Slaves certainly were not provided any concrete information about what was earned from their labor, and sharecroppers, at least in our situation, also were not informed about the profits derived from their work on the farm or the charges that were taken out of their share of those profits. In both cases, critical information was kept hidden, demonstrating a lack of respect for the people doing the work and a sense of superiority over them.

The similarity also extends to the reality of not living with a viable choice. Slaves certainly had no option at all regarding where they lived and who they worked for. Sharecroppers did have a choice, at least superficially, but was it really a choice for folks like my grandfather? For sharecroppers like him, you lived in the house provided by your landlord and you knew that you really couldn't afford to live anywhere else. So it didn't *feel* like much of a choice.

Of course, the major difference between sharecroppers and slaves was that slaves were literally owned by the family they worked for. They were human beings in bondage. As sharecroppers, the landlord didn't own you. Yet in some ways, you *felt* owned. You lived in a house they owned. You shopped at the store they owned, and you were charged amounts of money that the landlord did not have to reveal. You worked on the fields they owned. You used farm materials and equipment they owned and provided, again for a price that was not known by you. The landlords didn't own you by right of purchase, but they owned you by right of employment and labor.

You lived within sight of your landlord's home, but it was always clear that you did not live the same life. To me, the homes of all the white landowners in our area were mansions, even though they would probably be considered by other standards as comfortable but relatively modest dwellings.

Gaining this broader perspective about the circumstances of our family's life situation, I found myself calling upon a new name for it: *modern day slavery*. As Southern sharecroppers living on what felt like a plantation during the 1950s and early '60s, we were modern day slaves of that time. It was, in many ways, slavery without ownership.

I have another memory that reveals a great deal about the dynamics of our relationship with our landlords and those around them. I can recall several days when the owners of the farms near us would drive by our home early in the morning, before I had begun doing any chores for Daddy.

"Shade!" they would call out to my grandfather. "Can we use your boy today?"

And then I would go work for them in their fields, getting paid fifty cents an hour for my labor. I was their "boy." I imagine that my grandfather believed that he had no choice other than to say yes to this request, even if he did need me himself for tasks on our farm. If he had said "No, you can't use my boy today," and if he had added any remark about not wanting to have his grandson referred to as "boy" in the first place, he would have been asked to find somewhere else to live. Since he didn't have or could not afford anywhere else, he aligned with what was expected...in a way not so different from a slave.

What's so striking about the system of sharecroppers is that when you put together the details of what it was like and how it was structured and maintained, it reads like something out of the 1930s or '40s. And yet, this was our life in the years just before Martin Luther King came into prominence. It wasn't so long ago, and I was there.

By no means do I mean to demonize our landlords. They were human beings simply playing a role within a system that had not yet been dismantled. Interestingly, I have a photo that captures my first childhood memory. I am sitting on the front lawn of a house across from ours. The house was owned by our community's other major landlord, a family that treated us with kindness, even giving my grandparents something for our family now and then. From what I heard, however, they treated their own sharecroppers in the same spirit in which our landlords treated us.

None of this awareness was anything that we focused on back then. We were just intent on doing what we needed to do to survive. All year round we worked long, hard hours, without asking why.

In late summer of 1963, my grandfather and I were on the wagon off-loading corn at the pack house when he began to complain about having chest pains and indigestion. He kept working anyway, finishing the job just as he always did, no matter how he felt or how hot or cold it was. That's just who Daddy was. But when he went inside, he began feeling worse. Finally, Mama and Buddy got him to Trenton where he was examined by an old country doctor who just gave him something for the indigestion and sent him home. When the symptoms didn't go away, we were all worried. Eventually Mama found a way to bring Daddy into Kinston where a doctor took a closer look and assigned him to the hospital where African Americans were only allowed in the basement. He had suffered a heart attack.

A few days later, Shade Lane Roberts passed away. He was only fifty-five years old. It would not be a stretch to say that he worked himself to death.

Mama was now the sole decision-maker in our family. She was very clear about two important steps that we would take. "You are still going to finish high school," she told me. I was just starting my junior year at Jones High School. "And it's too hard for us to do this farming now. We will have to move somewhere else."

With no money or viable source of income, her options were limited. She turned to the only people she could count on: her family. We wound up moving into the nearby home of my uncle Buddy so I could stay in the same high school and graduate. At least we were freed from our life as sharecroppers, although I still performed paid labor in the fields. The village now sustained us. Later, Mama went to live with my uncle in his apartment in Kinston. I did finish high school, one of 101 graduates from Jones High School. Even my father took note of the occasion by giving me a graduation present which, if my memory is correct, was twelve pairs of socks.

Somehow or other, my grandfather had scraped together the money to buy a 1958 Ford Fairlane 500 not long before he passed. I had just learned to drive with that car and now it was mine. Did my grandfather somehow have an idea that he would soon be leaving me this car? I have often wondered about that.

For Daddy, being a sharecropper had given him life in the basic sense of having a home to live in and food to eat, but it also had contributed to taking his life through the long hours of demanding physical labor working a farm with primitive equipment. For myself, I also see both the drawbacks *and* the benefits that I took away from this experience.

It is true, for example, that although the hard work made me physically stronger at a young age, my body was also being damaged by all that manual labor. I began seeing a chiropractor to treat my back when I was only fourteen. He told me that I was born with a misalignment in my back and that I would need periodic adjustments. That may have been true, but I also believe that the demands of tasks such as bending over to pull the tobacco leaves and carrying heavy loads under my arms caused further, non-recoverable damage. To this day, I still have problems with my back.

It is also important to remember the unfairness and injustice that were part of our lives. Just adding transparency to the accounting of our income and charges would have gone a long way in making that sharecropper system at least a little more fair. But the simple truth was that families like ours were being mistreated and used, and we had no real choice about accepting it. And no one seemed to care.

But that's just the way it was back then. It's part of who I am and who I have become, and there were definitely positive influences that came from it. To me, there is always goodness that comes from any difficult situation or even a disaster. You've just got to find it. Growing up in a family of sharecroppers is simply something that happened to me in the past, something that helped propel me to do something greater in the future, an experience that now enables me to relate to others in similar situations so that I may assist them in finding a way out.

Working as a sharecropper certainly made me stronger mentally. From an early age I learned the value of hard work and gained an understanding of how to do things to take care of myself. I still remember Mama's lesson about the contribution I was making by helping my grandfather chop wood to fuel our home and hunt rabbits to eat.

Life on the farm also taught me a great deal about discipline. Growing and harvesting tobacco and corn, and all the other tasks I participated in, carried many physical and mental demands. I had to learn to endure those hardships, to stick with whatever I had to do even when it was hard. I gained a greater appreciation for how to accept the responsibility of doing something and seeing it through until the end. Completing the assignment was the expectation and there was no room to slack off. The mission had to be fulfilled. And after each challenging assignment was successfully completed, I learned something else: when the next task was given to me, getting the job done was not as difficult. I knew what was needed to achieve success and trusted my own ability and endurance.

These were all vital lessons that would serve me throughout my military career and in other endeavors in life. I appreciate them and have carried them with me, just as I have held onto the values instilled in me by my grandparents and the village that nurtured me. So you could say that my life lessons on our sharecropper farm could be called the "Wisdom of Modern Day Slavery."

3

THE WAY OUT...AND UP

I KNEW ONE THING about my future when I graduated from high school: college was not going to be a viable option. I had one meeting with my guidance counselor in which he indicated that he might be able to obtain an agriculture-oriented scholarship for me. The amount was $300. Well, with thousands of dollars needed each year for tuition, room and board, and books and supplies, that $300 was not going to go very far. I would need another plan.

I could have tried to stay in the Jones County and Kinston area, where I would have been welcome company and support for Mama in her adjustment to life without Daddy. The options there weren't too promising, though. My Uncle Walter told me that he could find me something where he worked at Smith Concrete in Kinston. Buddy had been working for years as an auto mechanic. Around home in Jones County, he would fix my grandfather's car and other cars in our family. When he wasn't tinkering with some old car, he would be out racing with friends. He left Jones County to work for a Chevy dealer in Jacksonville, North Carolina but had recently come back home to work as a concrete finisher. Following his tip, I did obtain a job at that concrete plant soon after I graduated. I was getting paid a little more than $10 per day, which was more than I made in the tobacco fields. But I knew that this employment was only temporary. I was being called in a very different direction, and answering that call was going to mean traveling much further than the short drive to Kinston.

My future would be navigated wearing the uniform of the United States Air Force.

Unlike a large percentage of Air Force recruits these days, I didn't make this choice after spending a great deal of time around an Air Force base to get to know something about what it was all about. Seymour Johnson Air Force Base in Goldsboro was only about twenty-eight miles away, but I had never even visited it. I didn't know much about the base's history—how it had been established during World War II and served as a training center for the P-47 Thunderbolt pilots who were instrumental in turning the air war in Europe in the Allies' favor. I was not aware that it was deactivated after the war but then reopened in 1956, or that it housed B-52 bombers. I was more familiar with Fort Bragg Army post in Fayetteville and Camp Lejeune Marine Corps Base in Jacksonville, about thirty minutes from us. Sometimes the Army would conduct maneuvers in our area.

The idea of a military career as a way out of poverty came from the same source of most of my major influences in life: my extended family. Two of my cousins were instrumental in blazing the trail that would point me toward my long and fulfilling career serving our country.

Interestingly, my first example of a potential military career was not linked to the Air Force. My cousin William McBynum and his family lived just a few hundred yards down the road from us and worked as sharecroppers for the other primary landlord in town. Even though William was ten years older than me, I related to him more like a brother than a cousin. When William reached the threshold of adulthood, he too had been searching for a way out of the sharecropper way of life. The U.S. Army provided him that chance. Here's how William explains it:

> I remember something our high school graduation speaker told us. He said "He who thinks he can, can." From the time I was sixteen I had been learning about other places that I had never been to and I had a yearning to discover more, to find something better than the life I was living. Before then, everything seemed good. I knew we were poor, but we had enough to eat and we were a close-knit, loving family. But now I had new horizons in sight, and I decided to join the military to get there.
>
> It wasn't easy. My mother wanted me to go to college, even though we could not afford it. She had always been the one to emphasize the need for education. My father wanted me to stay home because I was a good laborer and an important helper for him in the fields. Because I was seventeen when I made my decision, and my parents would not sign for me to join the military, I had to wait until I turned eighteen. I registered for the draft and also volunteered, and before I knew it I was off to Fort Jackson in South Carolina for basic training in the Army.

William trained as a medic and, after encountering initial obstacles, he decided to leave the Army after fulfilling his two-year commitment. He didn't stay out long—less than two months later he re-enlisted. He went on to earn his nursing license and served a stint in Korea before he was assigned to Special Forces and stationed just down the road from us at Fort Bragg. He would come back to Jones County often, and he made quite an impression on young men like me.

"I had money and a nice car, and I was very popular with the young ladies," William recalls. "I would talk to all the young guys in the area, those whose families were poor, and tell them the military was absolutely the best thing they could do."

William derived special satisfaction from sharing a story about showing off one of his cars. He had purchased a brand new Buick LeSabre and was driving it around Jones County one weekend when he spotted the car of a member of the family of his landlord parked at a small grocery store. William pulled right up alongside that car and waited. When the young man who had known William for years, and who had been above him as a member of the landlord family, came out of that store and saw who was behind the wheel of that shiny new car, his jaw dropped open. Greeting him with a smile, William said, "You thought I was going to be riding a tractor all my life, but guess what? They'll sell us a car too, if we have the money." He may have used more descriptive words to drive home his point, but I will leave it at that.

William made a major impression on me. So did my cousin James, who grew up in the country near us but in a family that owned property and was therefore not as mired in poverty as we were. James' father and my grandfather were brothers. He was only a few years older than me and was in my brick masonry class in high school. I always admired James for his intelligence and, since his family had more resources than ours, I always expected him to do great things. He had chosen to join the Air Force and was having a very positive experience as an aircraft mechanic when I was closing in on my decision-making time.

"Man, there must be something about being in the military that's pretty good," I said to myself. "These two guys seem to be doing very well."

James made a direct pitch for his chosen branch of the Armed Forces.

"You should definitely join the Air Force," he told me. "You will learn a lot and gain many new skills. With your ability in Business Math, they might find you work in that area in the Air Force."

That advice certainly made sense, but I have to admit that James' pitch was not the only reason I would opt for the Air Force. I had been hearing stories about William's life in the Army much longer, and much of what he described also appealed to me—except for one part. He had to spend many hours conducting dangerous-sounding maneuvers deep in the woods.

"I think I'll try the Air Force," I concluded. It wasn't just a question of staying out of the woods. I also regarded the Air Force as the best opportunity for me to pursue my goals. The Air Force was known for excellent technical programs, and I liked what James had said about using my skills in Business Math. Perhaps I could work in accounting someday.

Choosing to enter the military was also consistent with my desire to be of service. Even as a teenager, this was an important consideration for me. Driving a school bus at the age of sixteen had been a responsible thing to do, and I knew that I was helping children and helping our community. Of course, I was also helping myself because it gave me $30 per month that I otherwise would not have had. The military could work the same way: I would be serving something greater than myself while also improving my own life situation. I was ready to take this step. William was glad to see me choose a military career but just a little disappointed that I was not joining the Army.

"I have to admit that my perspective about the Air Force and those who were in it back then was that they were a bunch of sissies," William laughs. "The Army was for the rough-and-tumble guys like me, and I wanted anyone that I was personally recruiting to become a part of it. Of course, when I had the opportunity to serve alongside the other branches in Vietnam, I learned that the Air Force, the Navy and the Marines were excellent forces, too. We were all equal really."

When I made that decision to join the Air Force in the summer of '65, I was still only seventeen. That meant that Mama would have to sign her okay for me to join. This was not an easy thing for my grandmother to do. Not only was she still grieving the loss of her husband, she also had just undergone her first round of treatment for breast cancer. She really would have liked the comfort and support of having me around. At the same time, from the day she first held me by that old heater in the middle of our living room to keep me alive after my premature birth, Mama had always been committed to doing what was best for me. She knew I was not where I wanted to be in my life. I also tried to reassure her that entering the military and having a solid and reliable income would enable me to better provide assistance for her. I was going to do everything I could to take care of her after she had exhibited so much love and caring in raising me.

There was one other important factor in Mama's considerations. She had witnessed the example of other relatives who had decided to join the military but then wound up coming right back home after flunking their physical. William's brother, who also happened to be named James and who lived right around the corner from us, was one of many who had that experience. So when Mama finally agreed to sign for me, she may well have been telling herself that I was going to be sent back to her right away because of a problem detected with my back or some other physical condition.

It was early on the morning of August 4, 1965, when Mama, Buddy and my mother drove me to the Trailways bus station in Kinston. In my life up to that point I had never been further than one outing to Washington, DC with a church group. Now I was headed to Raleigh and the military processing center there, and if I *did* pass my physical I would be flying off to San Antonio, Texas for basic training at Lackland Air Force Base.

The bus ride to Raleigh was about seventy miles, and when I arrived at the induction station I was amazed to find the long, long lines of recruits waiting to be processed. I was not used to being around so many people! After I took my physical, it was another long wait until we would be informed of the results. That gave me time to think about what was happening.

I was leaving the only home environment I had ever known. I was leaving behind those mules! I was leaving behind the thought that I might be stuck in Jones County and mired in poverty the rest of my life. And in moving forward, I was going to have the opportunity to earn an income and, hopefully, gain a further education. I would have the chance to better my own life while also helping to provide a better life for my grandmother.

The results came back. I was accepted! After I was sworn in, it was time to call home. I was excited about what lie ahead but also sad. This news was going to break Mama's heart. She told me that she understood that I was doing what I needed to do. Her unconditional love for me had never wavered before and nothing would change that now. Had Daddy still been alive, I feel confident that he also would have supported my decision. My grandfather's love for me and his desire to see me achieve more than he could himself was strong.

I had never been on an airplane before, so the Eastern Airlines flight from Raleigh to San Antonio was going to be another new adventure. I handled that experience easily enough and felt comfortable and confident when we landed at the San Antonio airport around 10 p.m. There was another huge processing station there, but after managing that scene in Raleigh I was ready for the lines and the waiting. Finally, we were directed to board a bus for the twenty-minute ride to Lackland.

On the bus, I got my first taste of what the eleven weeks of training were going to be like. First, I noticed that while some recruits were African American, many more of them were white. Coming out of segregated schools in Jones County, I was not used to entering an intense environment with so few minorities. And the man who stood up in front of the bus to address us *definitely* did not look like me. This red-haired man was a Technical Sergeant, and he was going to be our instructor during basic training.

"Look at me," he began. "I am your mother, I am your father, I am your brother and I am your sister. For the next eleven weeks, I am going to be your *everything!*"

I can still see that Sergeant's face. For some reason, I thought of Donald Humphrey, a white kid who lived in a home a short walk from ours. Donald and I used to work side by side in the tobacco fields, and we never had any problems. In fact, I looked at him as kind of like a brother. And despite the injustice of the share-cropper system with the white landlords and African American workers, we actually never had any outward problems with race in the country. We would hear about racial tensions in the cities on our old black and white TV, but I couldn't relate to it personally. So I really wasn't troubled by the color of the man who was going to be my "everything." However, I sure wasn't used to someone being so intense, so up close and personal. But this was the military. I had entered another world!

He's in charge, I thought to myself, *so whatever he says must be true. I'm going to have to obey him and anyone else who gives us orders, and I'm going to have to do my best every day. And even if I don't like something, I need to remember that this too shall pass. I know a thing or two about how to face adversity.*

Lackland was huge, much bigger than what I had anticipated. I was soon introducing myself to young men from all across the South and all over the U.S. Some of them looked and acted nervous, but once I had recovered from the initial wake-up call on the bus I found myself feeling calm, peaceful and prepared for whatever came my way.

Fortunately, that attitude held up for the entire eleven weeks. While some recruits struggled with the regimen and the orders, I adapted easily. I could see right away that the discipline I had learned back home was going to be invaluable in this new environment.

"Being in the Air Force is like working on the farm," my cousin James had told me. "There is work to be done and if you do it, you will succeed. It's all about doing what is expected and getting along with the people around you. And don't worry if you don't know how to do something. They will teach you what you need to know."

I recognized that to make it through basic training, I just had to pay attention, listen closely, understand what was being asked of me at every turn, and do it thoroughly and completely. It was a matter of just doing the right thing and following orders. I also would need to accept the long hours and the lack of personal freedom. Being familiar with all of these requirements, I knew that basic training would not serve as any kind of obstacle for me.

Many of the other recruits couldn't cut it. For some, it was a matter of poor physical conditioning. I wondered how some of them had even gotten in, but the war in Vietnam had begun to heat up and recruiting had to be accelerated because the military needed more troops. Others had a hard time because they were so far from home, or they just weren't used to the raised voices of the instructors and the constant need for discipline. Some wound up getting sent back home.

While basic training was not so difficult for me mentally, I admit that it was challenging for me physically. Yes, the long hours of manual labor on the farm were strenuous, but you were mostly working on your own there. Now, in my first experience in the military, I had to learn that you can't always do it by yourself.

Many of our training exercises presented a problem requiring teamwork. You were given a task that you simply could not accomplish on your own. To succeed, you would have to rely on your partner and others around you. As an example, we were brought to the front of a climbing wall and told that all of us would have to climb over it. We could see right away that there were no steps or ledges to help get over the wall, and no rope to propel you. After awhile I figured it out: the only way for us to get over that wall was to use one another's support. One by one, we would get up on each other's shoulders until we could rise close enough to the top of that wall to pull ourselves over it. We made it because we worked together as a team.

Worn out from the day's activities, I had no trouble sleeping in our basic barracks. The food was more than sufficient and late in the evening I was comfortable keeping mostly to myself, alone with my thoughts for the future. Others around me may not have been so committed to a long career in the Air Force, but I had specific goals from Day One. The good Lord willing, I was going to stay in the Air Force until I retired. This really was going to be my life's work. I had heard that you could retire after twenty years of service if you did well, and with visions of those old gray mules and the sharecropper experience still vivid in my mind, that sounded very appealing to me. I did *not* want to go back to Jones County and a life of poverty.

The specific image I held in my mind was of retiring as an E9: Chief Master Sergeant. Little did I know that I would not actually achieve that mark, but I would climb a whole lot higher! Of course, the process of rising through the ranks would not come for quite awhile.

Today, as soon as recruits complete basic training they are usually sent off to technical training. That was not true in my day. Before reporting to Lackland, I had taken the Armed Forces entrance exam. I scored in the eightieth percentile in administration but only in the sixtieth percentile in general aptitude. Those scores determined the kind of assignment you would receive out of basic training. With my love for Business Math, I was hoping to be placed in Accounting. Instead, I was ushered into general work in the areas of supplies, food services and other basic tasks. I went Direct Duty to my first assignment from basic training, which meant you learned on the job. I was going to be sent to Grand Forks, North Dakota where I would be working in a warehouse. That sure didn't sound like a very glamorous position, but I was not complaining. This was just going to be my first stop as an airman, and there would be many more stops to get where I wanted to go.

I was able to fully soak in the glorious graduation ceremony held every Friday morning for 500 or more recruits on the large open parade field at Lackland. I had no way of knowing that this was to be the first of dozens and dozens of graduations I would attend at this same site over the course of the next several decades. But this day would always be special because it was *my* graduation, my official entrance into service in the Air Force.

Unlike most of my fellow airmen I did not have family members there to witness the big event and the entire weekend of activities scheduled for airmen and their loved ones. Mama would have loved to have witnessed my graduation, but she could not possibly afford to pay for the transportation to Texas. That was part of the reality of living in poverty: you could not do what you might really want to do, or go where you felt you needed to go.

However, I really didn't mind that my grandmother couldn't fly out to San Antonio to be with me. As I took the oath to become an airman, Mama was fully present in my heart.

CHAPTER

4

IT'S ALL ABOUT ATTITUDE

IF THERE IS ONE THEME that I emphasize more than any other when I talk to young people today, it is this: no matter where you are and what you are asked or expected to do, your success will almost always depend on your attitude. When I look back at my first experiences in the Air Force as a newly-graduated airman in the mid-1960s, I can definitely say that it was my attitude that propelled me forward in the direction that I needed to go.

Before reporting for my first assignment, I was granted a one-week leave to go back home to North Carolina. I welcomed the chance to spend time with Mama again, but leaving this time was even more difficult than when I departed Jones County to report for basic training. Our bond was just so strong. I knew that I would miss her and she would dearly miss me, but I held firm to my goals: to make a better life for myself and to earn enough money to provide for my grandmother. I was already thinking about buying Mama a house someday so she would no longer have to rely on the generosity and kindness of other family members to sustain her. I wanted to give back to her because of all that she had given to me.

After a week of vacation in North Carolina, I boarded a bus for the long trip to the Grand Forks Air Force Base located north of Emerado and west of Grand Forks, North Dakota in the heart of the Red River Valley. By then it was already December of '65, which meant that my new home was going to be cold—very cold. For a young man still a few weeks shy of his eighteenth birthday who had never ventured north of Washington, DC, this was a major shock to the system. The first article of clothing we were issued was a huge parka with a hood to cover your face.

"What are we going to do with this?" I asked innocently.

I would discover the answer to that question soon enough. Even before I had to spend much time outside in the elements, I was given another clue about what I would be dealing with. We were informed that the only way we should attempt to get from our dorm to the dining hall was to walk in the snow tunnel that had been built on the base. A *snow tunnel?* I soon found out that on those rare occasions when temperatures reached as high as thirty degrees, it was cause for celebration: you could wear a short-sleeve shirt!

As I sought to get acclimated to my drastically different living environment, I also had to learn my military occupational skill: supply warehouseman. I was introduced to my supervisor, a Staff Sergeant, and the civilian boss of the warehouse. Another civilian assumed the role of my hands-on trainer. He had a serious and somewhat sour manner but I got along with him just fine. I understood that he just wanted to ensure that everything was done correctly, and with my discipline gained from working on the farm and driving a school bus as a teenager, I had no problem meeting his expectations.

It didn't take long for my superiors to note my commitment and dependability. "We'll keep you moving right along," the supervisor said. From his perspective, the Staff Sergeant chimed in, "Flowers, you'll do fine in the Air Force."

I believe that I made that kind of impression because of my attitude. It was clear that many of my fellow airmen in the warehouse regarded the work we were expected to do as beneath them, even degrading. They would see the other young men in our dorm go off to work in the offices, wearing their clean pressed blue uniforms, while they came home all scuffed up with dirty shoes from another day moving things around in the dusty warehouse. "I've got to get retrained to do something different," they would say through their behavior and demeanor. "It's not fair that I should be asked to do this work."

My attitude was different. Through my actions and the way I carried myself, I tried to communicate this message: "If I am going to be a warehouseman, I am going to the best warehouseman around."

Yes, I was doing manual labor, but I was used to that. And I was being well compensated, at least by my standards. On top of free room and board, we received $94 a month in pay. That translates into more than $1,000 per year. It's true that in the civilian world I might have been able to obtain a job somewhere like a General Motors plant and be making $100 or more per week, but that was not something on my radar. I just knew that as sharecroppers, even in one of those rare years in which Daddy made any profit at all, his income for a full year of labor was probably no more than $300. So I had more than tripled my income. Beyond that, I was living in a dormitory that the taxpayer was paying for, and I was being well fed. What could I possibly complain about? And because I was disciplined enough to stay in the dorm for almost all my meals, and not waste money on outside entertainment, I was able to put $30 of that $94 every month into the credit union to save for my own future and to move closer to my goal of buying my grandmother a house.

My two roommates were making different choices. One, who happened to be white, was a Californian who came from a fairly well-to-do background: beautiful house, expensive clothes, new car. He was always receiving boxes from home with nice things inside. When the weekend came, he was ready to go out looking for a good time. I couldn't relate to him or his world at all.

My other roommate, an African American from Memphis, was a musician. He played bass guitar in a little band that sometimes performed on our base. They also landed paying gigs off base, so whenever he got free time he would be away playing or rehearsing. I remember him heading out in his little Chevy Corvair as his band headed to downtown Grand Forks or on longer excursions to Minneapolis or Chicago. Both my roommates called me "Country" and teased me for sticking so close to base. I didn't mind at all.

There were a fair number of African Americans at Grand Forks, although our numbers were not as strong as the African American representation in the Army and Marine Corps. At that time, the Air Force and Navy were seen as the branches of the military with more stringent entry requirements. During this period of escalating racial tension in the culture, we had our taste of unrest as evidenced by the occasional race-triggered fights in the dining hall. For the most part, however, blacks and whites found a way to peacefully coexist and work together.

I was not the only African American who had come from a poor background. There were many of us who had chosen the Air

Force as a way out of poverty. Interestingly, there seemed to be a noticeable difference between those who grew up in rural areas of Southern states such as South Carolina, Georgia, Alabama, Louisiana and Mississippi, and those who came from the big cities in the North or Midwest. The city guys had worked in factories or in the retail industry, and they held different views than those of us from the country. On weekends the city folks liked to cross the Canadian border to go drinking and running around with women in Winnipeg. The country guys tended to stay in the barracks and study for their skill exams or look for other ways to advance their careers. We didn't have any problem with foregoing the good times because we knew how important it was to work hard if you wanted to better yourself. We understood that who you are and where you come from has a lot to do with where you're going and how you'll get there. Again, it's all about attitude.

For a base in such a remote location, Grand Forks played an important role in Air Force operations. It was established in the mid-1950s as an Air Defense Command fighter-interceptor air base, a vital function during the height of the Cold War. In 1967, the Department of Defense revealed that the Grand Forks Air Force Base was one of ten initial locations to host a Sentinel Anti-Ballistic Missile (ABM) site.

As I continued to earn the trust of my supervisors and take on greater responsibility, I was put in charge of the base's war-readiness storage supplies and materials. In this area of the warehouse, it was critical that everything was stored in exactly the right place at all times. When someone needed a particular supply for a missile or an aircraft, you had to quickly and accurately locate it and deliver it to the airplane or other destination expeditiously. This was another task that I was able to master without problems or complications. Just as it was in Jones County, I had proven myself to be someone that could be consistently relied upon.

In the late summer of '67, several of us were selected to involuntarily retrain in air transportation and sent to Sheppard Air Force Base in Wichita Falls, Texas. Sheppard was an especially busy training center for operations related to the Vietnam War. It hosted the training of pilots for airplanes and helicopters, and the Strategic Air Command conducted aerospace rescue and recovery schools there. Our mission was to learn to load and unload airplanes with cargo. By January 1968, just after turning twenty years old, I was sent to Vietnam.

Assigned to Da Nang Air Base, I was walking into a major hot spot at a time when hostilities between North and South Vietnam were dramatically on the rise. Da Nang had established itself as a major center of operations for American forces, critical for launching air operations over North Vietnam. It was also a vital center for sending out recovery units. That's the activity I would be involved in.

As it turned out, my arrival happened to coincide with the launching of the first Tet Offensive by the North Vietnamese in late January 1968. The Tet Offensive was one of the largest military operations in the entire war. The Viet Cong and North Vietnam's People's Army of Vietnam coordinated a surprise attack, timed around the Vietnamese New Year, in more than 100 strategic locations throughout South Vietnam. It significantly ramped up American involvement and was followed by other Mini-Tet Offensives in the ensuing months.

There I was, having just completed adolescence, right in the thick of it all. I remember my brief visit with Mama just before I departed for Vietnam. She had heard that one of William's cousins, Jimmy, had been killed parachuting into enemy-held territory. Like me, Jimmy had been recruited to join the military by William.

Although obviously fearing for my safety, Mama bravely said, "We'll keep you in our prayers. You'll be fine." While continuing to battle her own scary health issues, she also declared, "But I won't be here when you get home." As it turned out, we both got through those trying times successfully. I made it safely out of Vietnam and went on to serve more than forty additional years in the Air Force, and my grandmother would live to be ninety-eight!

Oh, but there was danger, and the heightened tension would take its toll. During my first night in Da Nang, we were hit with a rocket attack. I had never been in combat before and had very little idea what it was all about. When the sirens went off, and the rockets came in, and everyone was running around with their helmets, fight jackets and weapons, I didn't know what to do. When I noticed that the others all seemed to be running in the same direction, I said to myself, "Well, I should just run where everyone else is running." That turned out to be a bunker, something else I was not familiar with. But I stayed hunkered down in that bunker with everyone else until we received the all-clear, and then we headed right back to our tent.

As I would soon discover, this was not a rare occurrence. For the next several months in Da Nang, there were very few nights in which a rocket attack *didn't* happen. We all slept in a flak jacket and helmet, with an M-16 stationed by our beds, because you didn't know what you might be called on to do. During those long, loud nights, we lived in fear as Da Nang earned the nickname "Rocket City."

I was assigned to the Aerial Mobility Team and trained to handle cargo in the C-123 Provider, the C-130 Hercules and the jet-powered C-141 Starlifter. I had only been in Da Nang a few weeks when I was awakened during the night for the first time for a live mission: go out and pick up cargo and "maybe some body bags."

We were flown to our destination, offloaded some supplies and then loaded our cargo. The C-123's could only fit three pallets, and one pallet was used for supplies. The other two pallets contained human remains. We brought them back to Da Nang, where they would be sent to the mortuary and prepared to be flown home.

Night after night, these excursions into the jungles and other war zones led us to a similar scene: bodies needing to be transported out of the battle zones and eventually back to their loved ones. We picked up other cargo, but it was the human cargo that left its mark. I tried to relieve the stress by drinking and smoking. It seemed as if everyone was drinking heavily, no matter what their backgrounds or beliefs were. I was not afraid of combat, and I did not fear death. Yet I have to admit that these operations really got to me. These were bodies of guys who were nineteen, twenty years old…just like me.

About six months into my combat duty, I developed a bleeding ulcer. I knew that it could be attributed not only to my poor lifestyle but to the horrors I was witnessing. I was treated first at the base and then at a military hospital in Cam Ranh Bay. Basically, they just patched up my stomach and sent me back to Da Nang. I was no longer assigned to go out on rescue and retrieval missions, with my assignment confined to the flight line at Da Nang.

During this period in Vietnam, I had initially hoped to have a chance to meet up with my cousin William, whose duty with the Army had taken him to Vietnam. Unfortunately, William suffered a worse fate than I did. His job as a medic brought him to another hot spot in the war: the Delta. As he would explain later, "I knew right away that I was in the wrong spot at the wrong time." He got hit by a mortar attack, resulting in serious injuries to his stomach, legs and chest, as well as shrapnel in one of his eyes. He wound up spending a whole year recovering from his injuries at Walter Reed Hospital back in the U.S.

My Vietnam assignment ended in January of '69. My time in the war was barely a year, but it left a lasting impact on me as the war experience did for most Vietnam vets. As I look back at that experience, I have to admit that I did not understand what the war was all about. I witnessed a great deal of fighting, destruction and death, and I really didn't know why we were there, why we lost 58,000 lives. I didn't ask "why" in the midst of doing my duty. I always did my job because that's what the Air Force had asked me to do and that is the attitude I always strived to live by. And yet, the lingering question of why would not go away....

I don't remember the year that I first visited the Vietnam Veterans Memorial Wall in Washington, but I vividly recall my profound sense of loss as I looked at the names I recognized, including William's cousin Jimmy. I also came upon many names I had read on the tags of the body bags we had picked up on our retrieval missions. I can still see myself riding on those cargo planes, including the C-130 that could fit six pallets. That meant there would likely be bodies being transported back with us to Da Nang.

Those feelings and memories are the same each and every time I go back to The Wall, but I don't have to go there to have those images stirred up in my mind. Just hearing a news story about the losses of Vietnam can impact me. It has been suggested to me that my response could be a sign of PTSD, but to that I say that almost anyone who was part of that experience carries a part of it with them. It's just the way it was.

Coming out of Vietnam, I was hoping to be retrained in accounting. I was retested and scored well on the administrative side, just as I had before, and approved for retraining. I was anticipating returning to Sheppard Air Force Base to learn my new skills, but that was not to be. With the war still in an intense phase, the Air Force had continued needs for air freight specialists, and when you commit to a military career you must maintain the attitude of fully accepting that the military's needs outweigh your own personal desires or wishes. I was to be reassigned to Norton Air Force Base near San Bernardino, California, and I was ready to take on whatever duties they entrusted to me. I kept in mind that when you have the right attitude, you never know what surprises may be in store for you.

Norton at that time was serving as a logistics depot and heavy-lift transport facility for a variety of aircraft, equipment and supplies as part of the Military Airlift/Air Mobility Command. It was one of only six Military Airlift Command strategic-airlift bases supporting Army and Marine Corps airlift requirements. Among other vital functions, the base supported Titan and Atlas Intercontinental Ballistic Missiles (ICBMs).

My individual assignment dealt with special handling cargo, such as guns and classified materials. I was in charge of an entire warehouse, a major step up from my role at Grand Forks. I appreciated these new responsibilities and focused intently on doing the best job I could do. But it would be something that happened on another front that made my stint at Norton memorable.

I noticed her right away, doing her work in the records and reports office in the same building I worked in. I found myself going out of my way to walk by her office and just sneak a peek inside where this attractive young lady and the other WAFs (Women in the Air Force) were seated at their desks. Of course, I was much too shy to consider actually stepping inside that office and introducing myself. I knew that I would need intermediary support, and fortunately it came from my friend Charles.

"Man, you're interested in that girl, aren't you?" Charles asked me when he caught me stepping slowly around her office. "Tell you what, I'll help you out here."

"How will you do that?" I asked.

"I know that she and her friends spend a lot of time in the bowling alley," he explained. "I'll set something up for the two of us and two or more of them."

Well, I did not know how to bowl because that was something else we couldn't afford back in Jones County, and I actually had no interest in bowling. But I agreed to the plan because I was highly motivated. I really wanted to meet and get to know that woman!

All I need to say about that night at the bowling alley is this: the mission was fulfilled. Her name was Ida and during our first dates I came to learn that her background had many similarities to my own. She was born in Mississippi and, like me, her parents did not stay together. Her mom was left to raise Ida and her five siblings, and it was a constant struggle. The family moved to New Orleans where they lived in what I called "jungle poverty", which may have looked different from the rural poverty I had experienced but had the common thread of economic, educational and social hardship.

I remember the first time I went to New Orleans to visit Ida's family. I caught a bus from the airport to a downtown hotel and then hailed a taxi for the trip to the ninth ward. When I told the cabbie the address where I was going, he said, "Do you know where you're asking me to go?" He explained that the area was called the Desire Projects and it was a scene of almost constant violence. "Put your bags in the backseat and be ready to grab them fast and get out when I stop, because I'm not getting out of this cab," he said.

That's the environment Ida had known, and like me she had turned to the Air Force as a way out. Yes, we had a great deal in common and got along very well together. It didn't take long for talk of marriage to drift into our conversations, and on June 22, 1969, we were wed. I had joined with the woman who would be my partner during the next forty-two years of my military career. There is no way I could have achieved the level of success I reached by myself, and I will be forever grateful for her partnership and her support.

She was the surprise that awaited me when I kept saying yes to whatever the Air Force asked of me.

5

LEARNING TO LEARN

LIFE AS A MILITARY COUPLE is not easy. Before we got married, Ida and I discussed all the questions that any military couple needs to consider before making a commitment. To what degree would the Air Force be amenable to assigning us to the same location and, if we ever did get separated by our assignments, how would we handle it? What would happen if we had a child, and what impact would growing up in an Air Force family have on our son or daughter? What else did we need to know about continuing our individual Air Force careers while joined as a couple?

We didn't have all the answers, but we were confident that we could face any situation that may arise as long as we maintained flexibility and a positive attitude. Well, it didn't take long for our resolve to be put to the test. Two weeks after we got married, Ida was assigned to Clark Air Base in the Philippines while I was accepted for retraining into accounting at Sheppard Air Force Base in Texas. In those days long before email and Skype, we were going to be separated by more than 8,000 miles.

Still, we held onto a trust that things would work out, that the separation would be temporary, and that we were both doing what we needed to do to advance our careers. For me, that meant embracing this opportunity to finally enter the financial side of Air Force operations. I could put my basic skills to use. I was on my way to move in the direction I really wanted to go in. The sky was the limit.

The only problem was, when it came time to begin the training I almost couldn't even get off the ground to launch my specialization. Something that I thought I would pick up fairly easily turned out to be hard, very hard.

For those first five or six weeks in accounting technical school, I just didn't get it. I applied my best effort in doing the work, but the numbers somehow were not lining up. For the first time in my life, I began to experience real doubt in myself. Going back to Jones High School, I had always done very well at everything that was put in front of me, or that I tried to do by my own choice, with no significant failures or setbacks. Now I was struggling. Late at night I would ask myself some tough questions: Is accounting and finance really the right thing for me, after all? Do I need to forget this dream and go back to air freight and stick with what I had learned and mastered in the Air Force? What were they going to do with me now?

Fortunately, during this time when I did not have the confidence that I needed to have in myself, someone else stepped in and demonstrated confidence in me. "Miss Leda" was the instructor that dedicated herself to pulling me through. "You can do this," she would say over and over. "You're just making simple mistakes." Then she would patiently point out how I had put a debit on the credit side or vice versa, or whatever I had done wrong, and urge me to get right back to it. She spent hours and hours of extra time assisting me. While I had been using my time thinking about what I couldn't do, she was using her time to show me that I could do it. By week seven of the training, the light came on. I was suddenly earning 99 or 100 on my tests. Everything just started to click, and my confidence in my ability to handle accounting was restored.

I have always remembered this devoted instructor. She helped me recognize that almost all of us will encounter some situation where we think we just aren't going to be able to cut it. When that happens, we need someone to put an arm on our shoulder and tell us "Yes you can." Decades later, after I had retired from the Air Force and was working in the private sector, I was supervising a woman in the accounting department who hit her moment of doubt. She was struggling in school while also working and raising two children.

"Don't ever doubt yourself," I told her. "Get the help you need and find the confidence to just continue on. When you continue on with your plans and your dreams, you never know where you will end up."

That's how it worked for me. I had found my passion, and my area of greatest potential, and it was off to the races in my Air Force career in accounting, finance and budgeting. After weathering that cloud of doubt, everything began looking up. Returning to Norton after successfully completing my retraining, I would soon hear more good news: my application for a joint spouse assignment had been accepted. By November of '69, I was packing my bags and heading off to the Philippines to join my wife at Clark Air Base.

I did hit a little snag, however. Instead of being assigned to accounting, where I had just proven myself, I got put back into air transportation at Clark. Once again, I had to accept that what you may *want* to do must always take a back seat to what the Air Force *needs* you to do. The Vietnam War was still very active and Clark served as an important logistics hub for war operations. Clark Air Base had been an important part of war history for decades. Early in World War II, the base was taken by Japanese forces and became a major center for Japanese air operations. Allied prisoners on the Bataan Death March passed right by the main gate to Clark. Later in the war, the Americans recaptured the base and maintained it as a strategic location on into the Cold War.

About six months into my time at Clark, I was able to land an assignment in the finance office there. My duties in air transportation had finally ended—unless the Air Force ever needed me back there again, of course. Ida and I completed our assignments at Clark in May 1971 and were sent back to Lackland Air Force Base in San Antonio, where she had been selected to be a military training instructor for women. I would continue working in accounting.

Our careers seemed to be advancing on a natural course when something else entered into the picture to shift the outlook. Ida was pregnant. In those days, women in the military in that situation had two choices: abort the baby or leave the service. Even if you were married, you could not remain on active duty and have a child. This was another one of those challenges that we knew we could face when we made the decision to come together as an Air Force couple. My wife had career goals, but there was nothing we could do about this. Policy is policy. Ida separated from the military. We accepted the situation and continued on.

On December 24, 1971, Alfred K. Flowers, Jr. entered this world. My wife settled into the role of staying at home with our child. And then, only a few months later, the military policy regarding women having children changed. If you were married, you could have a child and serve on active duty. Ida re-entered the Air Force and would go on to serve seven more years, and after leaving active duty she served with the Air Force Reserves for another decade and retired. So for quite some time, we were still very much an Air Force couple. Our faith that things would work out for us together in the Air Force was rewarded.

We would remain at Lackland until June 1972. Becoming the head of a family had an impact on my outlook for the future. It seemed even more important to continue to find ways to better myself, to improve my situation. Education loomed as a more compelling goal. No matter where I might go, it was clear that I needed an education beyond high school to get ahead. For a time, I wondered if I might need to leave the military to pursue a college degree. I even had thoughts about becoming a mortician, an idea shaped by watching my mother and step-father's partnership in a funeral home back home. At the very least, I decided that I should try taking a few college courses and see where that might lead me.

Once again, I hit an initial roadblock. One of the first courses that I enrolled in at San Antonio College was Invertebrate Zoology, a subject aligned with a potential move into the role of mortician. Just as I stumbled out of the gates in my accounting training, I got tripped up here. In fact, my grade for this course was a big F. I had done my best and I had failed.

This was another crossroads for me. I could have quit, just thrown up my hands and declared, "College is not for me!" I could have chosen to sacrifice my goals and settle for continuing along in the Air Force with only a high school education and limited opportunities for advancement. Or I could have decided to just go home and find something else to do to support our family.

That is not what I chose. After my wife and I were reassigned to Charleston Air Force Base in South Carolina, I discovered a new option for pursuing a college degree. Southern Illinois University offered a fully accredited degree program that could be undertaken and completed right on the base. You could take many classes on weekends, or attend some on weekdays if your supervisors were able to grant the time off. Sometime in late 1972, I enrolled full-time in a program aimed toward a Bachelor of Science degree in Occupational Education.

To be successful, I knew that I would need to perform much better in the classroom than I had in my limited educational ventures in San Antonio. As always, it would begin with the right attitude. Yes, I had failed a course, but in my mind I looked at it this way: failure is a speed bump to success. Rather than failing *backwards*, I would simply find a way to fail *forward*. I understood, even then, that as you seek to move ahead and better yourself, you need to learn from every opportunity and every challenge. You must approach life with a desire to do better today, and the next day and every day.

What lesson did I take home from failing a college class? I would have to do a better job at learning how to learn. I had to admit to myself that coming out of grade school and high school in Jones County, I really was not well educated. I benefited from the guidance of caring and dedicated teachers, but in the segregated schools our resources and methods simply were not at a very high level. That's the first step in turning any failure into future success: recognizing that there is something that you need and don't have, and then figuring out how to get it.

To succeed in college classes, I would need to learn how to read better and more thoroughly comprehend what I was reading. I came out of North Carolina with the habit of reading with my fingers, stopping over every word on every page. Over time, I learned that what you most need to know could be picked up by reading in a different way: paying more attention to the first line or the start and end of a particular paragraph or section.

I also recognized that I needed to improve in my ability to take tests. My enhanced reading and comprehension helped greatly in that domain, and I got better at identifying the material most likely to be included in any exam. To master the content I was studying, I made it a more regular practice to immediately look up any word I did not understand in the dictionary. That's a practice I continue to this day.

By committing to these new approaches to learning, I was able to stay on the path and complete my degree before our time at Charleston Air Force Base was completed in June 1975. I did not know it at the time, but this was only the beginning of a long trail of educational pursuits and achievements that would become part of my Air Force life.

One major benefit of obtaining any college degree is that it qualifies you for consideration for Officer Training School (OTS). That's something that was very much on my radar. If I could become an officer, I would have a much greater opportunity to continue to better myself within the Air Force. So even before I was awarded my degree, I had put in motion the process to apply for OTS, which was conducted back at Lackland. As soon as I had my bachelor's degree in hand, I was accepted into the program.

However, this invitation brought up a difficult choice. Around this same time, Ida was transferred to Iraklion Air Station on the Greek island of Crete. If I began and successfully completed OTS, I would come out a brand new Second Lieutenant, and with that status I would not be able to obtain a joint spouse assignment to be stationed in Crete. Officers are sent where they are needed. So my options were straightforward: 1) enter Officer Training School and then go wherever the Air Force needed me as a new officer; or 2) turn down OTS, remain an enlisted man, and seek a joint spouse assignment at Iraklion to stay with my family, leaving the matter of OTS on hold until I had the opportunity to apply again.

At that time, our son was three and a half years old. It was a critical time for our family, and family was very important to me. My wife and I had already been separated once for six months. As much as I wanted to become an officer, which would mean I would surpass my initial vision of retiring from the Air Force as a Chief Master Sergeant, I did not have to deliberate long over this decision. I would be heading for Crete.

Even though the journey that would finally lead me back to OTS would become more complicated and frustrating than I had hoped or imagined, I never regretted this decision. By then in life I had learned that in every situation you find yourself in, you have to know your priorities and stick with them, even if that meant sacrificing on another front. Living with my family was the priority here, and that's all that mattered.

We stayed in Crete for the next two years, and we had many wonderful opportunities as a family. Iraklion, located near the village of Gournes in the north central section of Crete, did not have the history of Clark Air Base. It had only been operational for about twenty years, but it fulfilled a vital role as host to the 6931st Security Group. I was able to continue my service in accounting, and my wife, my son and I found time to appreciate the beauty of the area.

For the first year or so, we stayed off base in a very nice apartment in Hersonissos, a city along the Mediterranean that was later developed into a major tourist destination. Living right on the ocean, we had ample opportunity to simply appreciate the beautiful blue waters. We also enjoyed being around the many friendly people on the island. It was a very different environment from the more insulated military bases that we had grown accustomed to calling home, and Al Junior got very used to having the beach as his playground. As he recalls:

"I remember walking out to that beach and asking my parents, 'Is every place we live in going to be as nice as this?' I loved picking up the seashells. I also remember that we had geckos and lizards running around our apartment. I had a broom to knock them down. It was fun. I also learned that people can look different or talk funny, but that's a good thing. It just reminds us that we all walk as one."

Of course, as parents Ida and I had other considerations beyond where to keep our son's seashells. We were both on active duty and when we arrived we knew no one in Hersonissos or on the entire island of Crete. We wound up meeting a family in which the wife was willing to look after Al Junior. After taking our son to the base with us every morning for the first week or so, we were dropping him off with someone who had been a perfect stranger. He spent all day with her.

Even though we liked our apartment, we decided that it was wiser to move onto the base as soon as we had the opportunity to do so. With a child almost ready to enter kindergarten, staying in a secure government environment seemed more responsible. At that time, however, housing at Iraklion was limited. The first real option was a trailer that was smaller than the home I grew up in Jones County. We accepted it and again had to seek someone to look after Al Junior. This time we wound up hiring a maid that also would assume child-care duties: taking Al Junior to school, picking him, up, watching over him, fixing his meals. She was a Greek national and, just as the woman who watched over our son off base, she had been a stranger until we hired her.

Although we were committed to our assignments and our Air Force careers, it's also true that my wife and I were navigating some of the more stressful terrain of life as a military couple with a child. We found ourselves placed in situations where we entrusted our son's care to individuals that we didn't really know, in an area far from home that we were just starting to figure out for ourselves. Fortunately, everything worked out fine, but we understood that it could have easily gone in the other direction. That's just part of the challenges that military couples routinely encounter. To outsiders, a husband and wife serving together and living together, all paid for by the taxpayers, may appear to be a sweet deal. Speaking from experience, it's not as easy as it looks. There were always stressors like this one that Ida and I had to work through. And because I had such a strong and committed partner, we always found a way.

For our son, living on the base at Iraklion, and on many other bases during his childhood, brought him into direct contact with the rhythm of life in the Air Force. It's a life he came to fondly appreciate.

"I loved our life—waking up to Reveille as your alarm clock, honoring the flag at the closing of the day at 5 p.m., and then 10 p.m. Taps," he explains. "I'm a proud military brat. I wouldn't have done anything differently in growing up. It built the fiber of who I am."

My wife and I are grateful that our son came away with those warm memories and that, as an adult, he would choose to continue the military way of life by becoming an Air Force officer in his own right.

So choosing to spend those two years in Crete was an excellent opportunity to continue to mold our family. It also offered me something else. Like the base in Charleston, Iraklion offered fully-accredited educational opportunities, this time through Ball State University's European division. By late 1975 I was at work on a Masters, continuing to apply what I had been learning about how to learn. I guess I must have been getting better as a student because well before we left Crete in June '77, I had earned a Master of Arts degree in Executive Development in Public Service.

All in all, that wasn't a bad accomplishment for a guy who had struggled mightily during the first five weeks of accounting school and managed to royally flunk one of his first college classes. With my commitment to regard failure as a speed bump to success, I was building a solid record of achievement both in the classroom and on the job. As I eagerly anticipated re-applying for Officer Training School, I couldn't wait to take on the greater challenges and increased opportunities to serve that would surely come with being an Air Force officer.

CHAPTER

6

No More Than
a Captain?

I DID NOT GET TO WHERE I ended up in the Air Force, retiring as a Major General, without encountering hurdles and roadblocks. The truth is that I came up against many obstacles and challenges along the way. That is part of the military life. Nothing is handed to you, nothing is guaranteed.

One of the major roadblocks in my path as an Air Force officer was just getting my foot inside the door. I had been accepted for Officer Training School in 1975 before I decided to turn down that opportunity in order to live with my family in Crete. But that didn't mean I had a standing invitation to just come on in and begin OTS any time I wanted to. Like anyone else, I had to re-apply and be assessed as if I were seeking entry for the first time.

I was hopeful and relatively confident of acceptance when I put the application process in motion before our assignments in Crete were completed. But when word came back, I learned that I had been rejected. As I sought to understand why, I discovered that I did not do well on the required AFOQT (Air Force Officer Qualifying Test). My score ranked below the threshold that candidates were expected to cross for serious consideration. Looking back, I don't know the results from the first time I took that test when I initially applied back in '75. Perhaps I performed a bit better then, or there may have been another contributing factor. I believe the Officer Training School quotas were higher at that time than when I re-applied.

I was disappointed by this rejection. After all, by then I had already earned a bachelor's degree and a master's degree. It was difficult to be turned aside because I had not performed well on one specific test.

Before I explain what happened next, allow me to offer my observation about tests like this one. Through my years of experience as a military officer, I concluded that tests like these may well be biased toward minorities. Historically, minorities have not scored well on the AFOQT. It's not hard to see why—many simply have not had the quality of education and training that others from different backgrounds had. That was certainly true in my situation. Yet that doesn't mean many of these individuals who test poorly can't learn and succeed as an officer, and in life, if they have the right attitude and the desire to achieve and excel. That's why, in recent years, I was actively working to change this system, perhaps using grade point averages or other metrics as criteria to select OTS candidates. I was not successful in seeking a change for this requirement.

In my situation, there wasn't much I could do about my test score and rejection, except to try again. I still lived by the belief that failure is a speed bump to success. I was confident that I could be a successful officer, but the only way to demonstrate that was to *become* an officer. I needed to find a way to get past the starting gate.

Coming back from Crete without that OTS acceptance, I was assigned to Travis Air Force Base near Fairfield, California. During World War II, Travis had served as a major aerial port and supply transfer point for the Pacific War Zone, and it was still a major hub for Air Force operations in the late 1970s. I worked diligently in my role as accounting noncommissioned officer, but my sights were still set at somehow transitioning into a career as an Air Force officer.

I decided to apply for the Medical Services Corps, a direct appointment program that I was eligible for because I had a Master's degree. I also had a strong business background, which was in demand at that time. But even this route presented a roadblock. I ran up against a general belief that candidates like me who had already served at least ten years in the Air Force would last no more than ten additional years as an officer and then leave to make more money in the private sector. They only wanted to invest in those who would stay longer. So there I was, an enlisted man who already had demonstrated the willingness to keep a long-term commitment, on the cusp of launching what turned out to be thirty-three years of service as an officer, being turned down out of an assumption that I would do only the minimum and then cut and run.

I was still not discouraged. You were allowed to re-apply for OTS six months after being rejected, and that's exactly what I did. And I was rejected again. I also tried the Medical Services Corps a second time and didn't make it there again, either.

I have to admit that at that point I began to have serious thoughts about my future, whether I might have a greater opportunity to better myself outside of the military. Those doubts were especially buzzing while I was training a brand new Lieutenant as part of my work at Travis Air Force Base. By that time, as Master Sergeant-select I was working quality assurance, checking to make sure that every staff member in our domain was handling the finance and accounting correctly and following all the relevant laws, rules and regulations. This Lieutenant that I was training had flunked out of navigator school and had recently been reassigned to finance. In my observation, he had a poor attitude, and despite having received a bachelor's degree he sure seemed to be lacking in intellect. I couldn't help saying to myself, "If this guy can be an officer and I can't, then maybe it really is time for me to do something else."

Even then, I decided that I was not ready to give up. I would apply for OTS one more time. And one more time, I was rejected.

It is with the utmost gratitude that I can report that this was not the end of the story. Someone would intervene on my behalf. Actually, it was not just one person but three individuals who stepped up for me at a time I most needed it. My immediate supervisor at Travis Air Force Base, a civilian, believed that I had potential as an officer and took the step of approaching the Colonel that we both worked for to speak on my behalf. He must have made an impression because this Colonel went right to our wing commander, Colonel Trott.

After hearing of my situation, Colonel Trott was willing to consider going to bat for me. However, since he didn't know me personally he wanted to meet me for an interview. I knew this would be a brief meeting, because he was a Colonel and I was just a Technical Sergeant, but I was eager to meet with him and answer any questions he might have.

"So why do you want to be an officer?" the Colonel asked when we sat down together.

"Sir, I believe I have much to offer as an officer and a leader," I began. "If I continue on as an enlisted man, I may have the opportunity to attain the level of Chief Master Sergeant, which was my goal when I enlisted in 1965. However, I would be limited in what I could give back to the Air Force for all that I have received. Being an officer would provide me more opportunities to offer everything I have to give."

Within days the Colonel wrote a letter to the key personnel administering the officer training program. I don't know exactly what he said in his letter, but from what I understand, after pointing to my qualifications and the recommendations of those who had served with me, he presented an argument that sounded something like this: Here's a person with thirteen and a half years of enlisted experience who has earned a bachelor's degree and a Master's and he can't be an officer because he didn't do well on a qualifying test? How many tests do you think he's taken and passed along the way?

Two weeks later I received word from OTS. "You have a class date," it read. My rejection had been changed to an acceptance. In August 1978, I was headed to the Medina Annex back at Lackland Air Force Base in San Antonio, the same place where I had gone through basic training. Only now it was for a new start in OTS.

That Colonel, someone who didn't even know me, recognized my potential from the information that was before him and the attitude that I demonstrated in meeting with him. I remain grateful for his intervention and always remembered his example. When I had the opportunity to lead and mentor scores of individuals as an officer, I always kept my eye out for where and when I could intervene on someone's behalf when I saw potential that somehow or other had not been recognized or acted upon. Unfortunately, many people don't see their own potential. Sometimes it takes others to help us identify our strengths and to encourage us, to stand up for us, to proclaim that there is more that we can offer, more that we can achieve, if we just have the opportunity.

With my goal of training to become an officer finally within my grasp, I was very clear about the attitude needed to go forward. My objective was to learn to be the best officer that I could be, and the best leader that I could be, and to eventually serve in the role of trusted and valued mentor for those that I was leading. In a basic way, it was really the same attitude I applied when I began my first assignment at Grand Forks thirteen years earlier, when I vowed to be the best warehouseman I could be.

As I began OTS, I also recognized that there was a mental adjustment needed to become successful. You can't say to yourself, "Well, I've been in the military ten years (or in my case thirteen and a half years) so I know all I need to know about the military." It is true that I had learned a great deal about military life, but I only knew about it as an enlisted man. I had never spent a day in my life as an officer.

There are some things you learn as an enlisted person that you can carry over to the officer side, such as customs and courtesies, drills and ceremonies, and all the do's and don'ts and rights and wrongs from the Uniform Code of Military Justice. To be an effective officer, however, you have to accept that you must be trained to be an officer. This was not a repeat of basic training. The expectations were very different. You had to learn to think like an officer, to carry yourself as an officer, to approach every situation you encounter as an officer. You were expected to learn ethical considerations as they applied to officers, not to enlisted men. You needed to learn the tenets and the responsibilities of command. You must always see the bigger picture of a situation, with an expanded scope of leadership. All of these teachings added up to a mental adjustment that many of my friends who had been enlisted men were not able to make.

Perhaps because of my attitude, or my long time of service coming into OTS, I was granted leadership opportunities right from the start. On the very first day of training I was approached by one of the commanders. "Hey, Flowers, you've been around a long time and you seem to know what you're doing," he said. "Why don't you take the flight to lunch?" There were twelve to fifteen trainees in each of six flights within the squadron of eighty to ninety officers in training. After the first six weeks of training, I became student squadron commander. It was a promising start.

I took these responsibilities and this great opportunity to become an officer seriously. My cousin William was living in San Antonio at the time, and on a day when we were granted a few hours to get off base, he invited me to his home for a barbecue. Here's how William recalls that day:

"It was a very hot day, and Al had his Air Force uniform on. I told him to at least take his shirt off, to relax, but he explained that he was expected to keep his uniform on at all times, even when he was off base. I said, 'Man, they can't see you here.' He just looked at me and said, 'But I can see me.' That sure made an impression on us."

I remember that day as vividly as if it had happened yesterday. It was December 3, 1978, two days before graduation. Not for one second did I have to stop and think about what I should do. It was simply a matter of doing the right thing and not the wrong thing, as I had always been told to do by my grandmother.

I completed OTS as a distinguished graduate and was commissioned in December 1978. My first assignment as a Second Lieutenant was as deputy accounting and finance officer at Moody Air Force Base, located near Valdosta, Georgia. A lot would happen for me in those next two and a half years at Moody. Early on, I was promoted to accounting and finance officer, and later I became the base's budget officer. The normal progression for a deputy is to serve for about two years before being entrusted with his own account. I had earned the trust to take that step in less than a year. We were responsible for the pay allowances for the staff of about 3,000 people at Moody, which had been the Southeast Training Center for the Army Air Forces Flying Training Command during World War II and was now host for the 347th Tactical Fighter Wing.

When I first made that progression to finance officer, I really began to recognize the change in serving as an officer. As a finance officer, you are responsible not only to your local leadership and your higher headquarters but also to the U.S. Treasury and to the American people for the caretaking of those resources entrusted to you. I could not have held that kind of responsibility as an enlisted person.

These were all important steps in the formative stage of my career as an Air Force officer. Yet it was two personal experiences that were especially impactful in fueling my desire to advance and excel.

The first one occurred after I was given the opportunity to attend Squadron Officer School at Maxwell Air Force Base in Alabama. It was a twelve-week school and the first level of professional military education for an officer. Attending that program helped open the door for my first promotion in rank, rising to First Lieutenant. What I remember most about this school was the feedback that I received after presenting a speech in one of my classes. I always wanted to perform at my best every day, and the effort that I had invested in planning and delivering this speech was consistent with that attitude. I believed that I had done the best I could, that my speech was grammatically correct and presented in a clear and confident voice. The class instructor, who was also happened to be one of my commanders, apparently saw it differently.

"You know, Flowers," he said after pulling me aside, "you've got a black accent. You may find that this will limit you as you seek to advance as an officer."

The words I would have spoken in response, had I allowed myself to address a superior in such a way, would have come out something like this: "A black accent? You think? Look at me. I've been black all my life. I don't even know what a black accent is but what you heard up there was...it was me. And if that's considered to be a black accent, I'm sorry, but that's all I've got."

Perhaps that instructor, who happened to be Caucasian, was from somewhere that people didn't talk at all like I did. I wondered if he had ever set foot outside the base there in the area around Montgomery, Alabama, because if he had, he would have discovered that most of the folks there sounded at least somewhat like me—even the white folks.

I could have raised a big fuss about this insulting remark. I could have allowed it to make me angry in a way that would distract me from the important learning made available there at Squadron Officer School. His remarks related to my race could have made me bitter.

But that's not who I was or who I am. Any time someone would make a disparaging comment like that or say something that indicated that they expected less of me than I knew I was capable of, I would take that comment and use it as further motivation to do better. Whenever I heard words that sounded like, "You know, Flowers, you don't quite measure up" or "We didn't think that was quite what we expected from you," I would always try harder. That's just my character.

Fortunately, I never heard this particular comment about my "black accent" ever again. As the years have gone by, I have even learned to laugh about it. But you can bet that I have never forgotten it. From that day on, I was determined to prove that guy wrong. I would never be limited or held back because of who I was, where I came from, or how I talked. Those kinds of roadblocks and challenges would not slow me down. You could bank on that.

The other personal experience that stoked my desire to excel occurred back at Moody. This time, it was a fellow African American who happened to make a comment that got my attention. And he didn't even make the comment to me. Our son Al Junior, who was then about eight years old, was playing with one of his buddies on the base, a boy the same age whose dad had entered the Air Force as an officer. The two kids came inside the other boy's home when the dad was there, and the dad got into a conversation with my son.

"You know, your dad won't ever be more than a Captain," he said. "Because of his long prior service before becoming an officer, Captain is as high as he will ever reach. No one will have to worry about Lieutenant Colonel Flowers. He'll retire as a Captain."

Al Junior was shocked by this prediction, and when he came home he told me about it right away. I looked at him sternly. "Okay," I said simply.

My son was old enough, and knew me well enough, to understand what that meant. I was determined to prove this fellow officer wrong. I had already made a commitment to myself to retire at a higher rank than Captain, to show others that just because someone happens to have served as an enlisted man for several years it doesn't mean they will be limited by rank or the duration of time in seeking to perform at their best as an officer. If that person did well, they could go higher. Education and training and the beginning curve of someone's Air Force career won't tell you what's in someone's heart. It won't tell you how motivated they are to achieve. This Captain and all the others would see that someday.

For the record, I achieved the rank of Major, the next rank above Captain, in less than ten years after this pronouncement. The years went by, and my promotions continued at a consistent pace, often ahead of schedule. One day I found myself in the company of this other officer again. He had retired as a Colonel and by that time I was already a General. I felt no anger toward him, no sense of superiority. After all, his remark was just another seed of motivation that helped me climb to greater and greater heights. I believe he felt remorseful about what he had said to my son that day, but that just made me remember a saying I had picked up while growing up in a family of sharecroppers in rural North Carolina: it's hard to separate good and bad water because once it's water, it's just all water.

So with the trust in me demonstrated by others and my motivation to excel, I was able to chart a consistent course through the ranks as Air Force officer. My dates of promotion offer an idea of my trajectory:

Second Lieutenant: December 11, 1978
First Lieutenant: December 11, 1980
Captain: December 1, 1982
Major: December 1, 1988
Lieutenant Colonel: August 1, 1992
Colonel: August 1, 1998
Brigadier General: September 1, 2004
Major General: November 2, 2007

There have been far too many assignments and meaningful experiences in my years as an officer for me to do justice to all of them here. I will do my best to touch upon a few highlights of what I did, and who I served with, as we go forward.

Many individuals made vital contributions that enabled me to work in diverse capacities and serve different communities and causes. At Moody Air Force Base, Major Ken Hotcaveg was instrumental in allowing me to diversify my responsibilities by moving me from accounting and finance to budget, and trusting me to manage my first account. The Air Force wants you to diversify your assignments during the early phase of your career as an officer, and I had an excellent opportunity to do that all within my first assignment.

Ken's leadership was an excellent example of an officer caring more for his people than himself. When we met, it was at a time when he happened to be uncertain about his next assignment. But he told me something that I will always remember. "Whatever happens in my career happens," he said. "But I'm going to make sure you have the best opportunities to be successful in your career." As a quick side note, Ken remained a trusted friend through all the years of my career as an officer. He made it a point to be in Montgomery, Alabama when I became a two-star general and then was in Washington at my formal retirement ceremony. He was one of many officers whose friendship and loyalty I would come to cherish.

Another officer who shaped my future during those early years as an officer was Allen "Doug" Bunger, who retired as a Major General. Doug is now deceased but will never be forgotten. I met him while attending a conference during my assignment at Moody. He took a liking to me then and sometime later, in June 1982, he invited me to come to Langley Air Force Base in Virginia to serve as a budget staff officer at Headquarters Tactical Air Command. I was given the responsibility of managing the $3 million Southwest

Asia account. That work often required me to spend time in the Pentagon, and when this officer wound up there he reached out to me again in 1985.

"Al, are you interested in coming to the Pentagon?" Doug asked.

"Sir, I would love to work for you again, wherever that may be and whatever I would be asked to do," I responded. "The Pentagon is just another place for me to perform and do my best."

I spent four years at the Pentagon that time, which would not be my last stop there by any means. The first two years I worked as budget analyst and then I served two more years as an executive officer to the Director of Budget Operations, a one-star General. That was a rewarding but demanding job. The officer that I worked for came to work at 5:30 in the morning, and he expected me to be there before he arrived. And I was. While he was consumed with his important round-the-clock meetings, our directors and I kept up with the mountains of paperwork associated with the job. When the General came out of his meetings around five o'clock, I would have anything that needed his attention ready and waiting. Then I'd stay with him another two hours or more to go over it all with him. Add to those long days the frequent demands for Saturday work and even a couple of hours after church on some Sundays and you've got a sixty-plus hour work week.

I welcomed the challenge, though, because I don't know of any other position where a young officer can learn more about how senior leaders act, react, think, strategize and accomplish things in the political powerhouse of Washington, DC. One lesson I especially learned was when you served in the Pentagon, your day is often controlled to a large degree by what's happening on Capitol Hill. You may begin a day going in one direction and then, after hearing of breaking news related to the budget, you might spend the next week trying to explain what really happened and articulate the facts, which were often not understood initially. So I got very used to being in the service of senior leaders that expect the execs to be there when they are, doing whatever needed to be done. Once you commit to that duty as executive, you've got to be ready to climb on that pony and ride it until it drops, or until you drop.

After that learning experience in the Pentagon, in July '89 I was given an opportunity in a different realm. Soon after being promoted to Major, I was going back to school. This time I was a student in the Armed Forces Staff College in Norfolk, Virginia. Attending this program was an eye-opening experience for me, because rather than being confined to Air Force personnel I was mixing with individuals from all the branches of the Department of Defense.

As an Air Force guy, you're always partial to your own service. You may think something like, "Yeah, the Army and Navy and Marine Corps are out there, and they have their mission and we have ours. But maybe we're just a little bit superior." Right from the start of this experience I came to understand and appreciate that each service was very good at what they do. It gave me a fresh perspective of the other services and the contributions that each one makes in serving our great nation. Some of my classmates went on to some remarkable achievements. I recall one who went on to retire as a four-star General.

While I was attending this program for six months, my family was still living up in the Washington, DC area, a few hours up I-95. My son recently reminded me of how I tried to maintain the family connection then. By this time, Al Junior had become an accomplished high school basketball player who would go on to earn a college basketball scholarship at Rider University. I didn't like missing his games, so on many occasions I would drive the three hours up to see him play, sleep a few hours at our home, then get up before 5 a.m. to make the drive back to Norfolk to arrive on time for my first class at 8 a.m. As the years went by, there were certainly occasions when I was not able to be present for important family events or experiences, which is something I regret. But in this situation, I was determined that when my son was playing the game he excelled at, I was going to be there to cheer him on.

Next I completed a long stint as Chief of Budget Operations of Air Combat Command back at Langley, which is located in the Hampton Roads area of Virginia. This assignment came during a time of reorganization of the Department of Defense that included Strategic and Tactical being joined to form Air Combat Command. Basically, two separate commands were integrated into one, creating many budgeting challenges that I enjoyed taking on.

From there it was back into the educational arena, first with the Air Force Air War College by seminar followed by the Industrial College of the Armed Forces, which would later be renamed the Dwight D. Eisenhower School for National Security and Resource Strategy. Through these programs I learned invaluable lessons. War College was certainly not a traditional kind of educational environment where somebody lectures you for three hours a day and then you do the homework, take a test and show up for more lectures. It was much more thought-provoking. You would be presented a hypothetical scenario that a leader might face and brainstorm how to solve it. As we discovered, there was usually no one right or wrong approach to take. While I wasn't commanding forces in war, these kinds of lessons expanded and enriched my sense of how I could operate as a leader.

I completed my course work in 1994 with a Master of Science in National Resource Strategy and Policy. For the next several years, my finance-related assignments alternated between Langley and the Pentagon. As Defense Resource Manager of the Joint Staff, I had the opportunity to build on my exposure to other branches of the service. I worked for Navy Admirals, a Marine Corps General and an Air Force General. During two years as Director of Budget Programs for the Air Force in the Pentagon, I worked directly for the Director of Budget. In that role, I was responsible for preparing budget briefings for the budget director, the Secretary of the Air Force, and Congressional presentations on Capitol Hill. I would build on that experience in the years to come.

By 2001, I had moved out of the Washington, DC-Virginia loop when I became Comptroller of the Air Education and Training Command at Randolph Air Force Base in San Antonio. We were responsible for basic training, as well as technical training and pilot training. In my role, I oversaw an $8 billion budget. I greatly enjoyed working with the dedicated and hard-working staff in the close-knit community at Randolph.

During all those years, I had been fortunate enough to be given a wide variety of assignments and responsibilities. In 2003, after rising to the rank of Brigadier General, I was selected for an assignment that took me in a very different direction. The news was delivered to me by my four-star boss who was the Air Education and Training Command Commander. We were on a flight to Dayton, Ohio together with business at the Wright-Patterson Air Force Base there.

"Al, I need to tell you what we're thinking," he said.

"Sir, whatever you're thinking, I'm thinking it's probably the right thing for me to do. I'm a servant," I responded.

"Well, another four-star is looking at you and we're thinking about sending you down to Special Operations Command to be the Chief Financial Officer," he explained. The General he referred to was commander of the U.S. Special Operations Command headquartered at MacDill Air Force Base near Tampa, Florida.

"Tell me when it's time to go," I said.

Soon after I returned to San Antonio, I was off to Tampa. My official role in Special Operations was Chief Financial Executive for the Center for Force Structure, Resources and Strategic Assessments, but I was soon promoted to director of that operation. It was an exciting experience to be involved with a program that brought together Air Force Special Operators, Green Berets, Navy Seals, the Marine Special Operations Forces and many other courageous and highly-trained personnel doing vital work for the security of our country during a critical period. During my time as director, I spearheaded the largest increase in resources and force structure for Special Operations Forces in the history of the U.S. Special Forces Command.

There would be other highly rewarding and unique experiences ahead before I retired, and I will focus on a couple of those in the chapters ahead. Looking back, I can say that my success and longevity as an Air Force officer can be traced back to that attitude with which I approached Officer Training School after I finally unlocked the key to the front door with the help of others who saw my potential and stood up for me. It bears repeating that no one knows other than you what's in your heart, what really motivates you to succeed. I was highly driven to serve as an officer and a leader, and to continue to better myself. And the roots of that fire and determination go back much further than OTS. It really came from my childhood and the values instilled in me by my grandparents in North Carolina.

From an early age, Mama and Daddy, and so many other folks back there in the country, taught me the right values: always doing your best, playing fair, doing what was right no matter what, paying attention at all times and simply understanding that there was a reason that you were born with two ears and one mouth. As I grew up, those values were nourished and expanded upon during adolescence and into adulthood, and then finally during my years as a military officer. Those values definitely served me well during OTS, when others were falling by the wayside, and they steered me through all those important assignments and promotions that followed.

Coming out of OTS, after thirteen and a half years as an enlisted man, I knew that I had a lot of ground to make up if I wanted to advance beyond the rank of Captain. I was getting a late start, but I was not deterred. I had witnessed many younger officers struggle to succeed, and I knew that I had the moral fiber, the drive, the motivation and the leadership ability to go further. My values, my attitude and the fire to excel burning inside me all came together and served as a springboard to take me where I was able to go.

Of course, there were many people, in so many places and positions, who did so much to help me along the way. Whether it was providing me the tools to break through some frustrating obstacle, or seeing something in me that others could not and guiding me toward a new and wonderful opportunity, these individuals made invaluable contributions to my story. In fact, without their guidance and support, there would be no story to tell.

7

TAKING COMMAND

IN MY FIRST TWENTY-EIGHT YEARS as an Air Force officer, I had earned an excellent reputation for successfully managing diverse assignments. All of them, however, were in the realm of resourcing. Then one day I was given an opportunity that financial guys like me never expect.

This time, I received the news while on a personal mission. It was late 2006 and my mother had just died. She had remained a strong supporter of my military career and was able to witness the pinning of my first star in 2004. I was spending time in Kinston and Jones County with my family, including my brother Uronus whom my mother had raised, when the call came from my boss, the Special Operations Commander and an Army four-star General.

"Al, I'm sorry for your loss and apologize for contacting you during this time with your family," he began. "I just need to let you know that I've been talking to some other Generals and I think we're going to send you to Maxwell. You're going to be the Commander of AFOATS (the Air Force Officer Accession and Training Schools)."

It took a moment for the meaning behind this new assignment to sink in. I had never commanded anything!

"Sir, if that is what the next assignment is, then I'm ready to go," I said finally. A few weeks after we returned from my mother's funeral, my wife and I left Tampa and drove off to Maxwell Air Force Base in Montgomery, Alabama. That's where I had first attended Squadron Officer School more than twenty years earlier when I was informed that my future would be limited because of my "black accent." I had become more familiar with the command in recent years because it was headquarters of Air University, a major component of Air Education and Training Command.

This was a truly exciting time for me because I had been afforded a very new and different opportunity. My attitude, even when I was still an enlisted man, was that being given an opportunity to perform and succeed was all you could ever want in life. Whether or not you took advantage of that opportunity was all up to you. And this was one opportunity that I was not going to let pass by without giving my maximum effort. As it turned out, this experience would be something I would cherish all my life.

The assignment came as something of a surprise because I had never been a squadron commander. It seemed as if any time there appeared to be a possibility of being assigned a command, I was needed to go back to the Pentagon for my next financial position. There were days that I would wonder whether I would ever have a chance to serve in this capacity. Well, I never did get to be a squadron commander, but that didn't prevent me from leaping ahead to serve as a *center* commander. And the Air Force Officer Accession and Training Schools, which has since been renamed the Jeanne M. Holm Center for Officer Accession and Citizen Development, was a huge operation.

First, it included the Officer Training School, which had been moved to Maxwell from Lackland Air Force Base in San Antonio after I had graduated from OTS. More than 500 officers would complete OTS every year. The center also held responsibility for Air Force ROTC, which encompassed 144 colleges and universities and some 12,000 students. Additionally, we oversaw the Junior ROTC programs, with about 115,000 students participating in 869 high schools in the U.S., with additional Junior ROTC outreach overseas.

I knew that I was taking on a major responsibility, and I recognized that in some ways I was going to be a fish out of water. With the vast majority of my previous assignments, I would enter into each new situation with a great deal of familiarity about what I would have to do and where I would be doing it. The most traumatic part of most of these moves would be the moving itself—packing up all our stuff and moving to a new place on short notice. Now I was stepping into a very different terrain, where instead of primarily leading financial and resourcing professionals, I would be leading several commanders and a large group of people. And there was no warm-up period here. I would be expected to be a highly effective commander on day one.

I would laugh later when reflecting on the reality of how officers are invited to step into major new responsibilities like this. "So here's what the Air Force needs you to do. You are a 'General Officer' and we know you will accomplish your mission. It is the best job you have ever had. Enjoy it starting day one because 'command' always ends early no matter how long you serve." That is how the message is often conveyed. Still, I was undaunted. I would simply take the same approach to leading these thousands of people that I had taken when leading three people. Keep it simple. Understand your mission, understand your people and give clear guidance. Remember that your people will always help you, one way or the other. They're either going to help you succeed or they're going to help you get replaced. So if you take care of your people, understand your mission, provide clear guidance and lead as a reasonable person who remembers that leading is not about you but about those you lead, you will successfully accomplish your mission.

I knew that in getting acclimated to my role, many talented and experienced individuals would be there to help me. Yet I understood that ultimately, I was going to be their leader. I was in charge. That's what we were taught from day one in OTS, and a major part of that difference between being an enlisted man and serving as an officer. You are in charge. Obviously I could not do it alone. I would need to create a leadership environment where people could clearly communicate to me about their individual jobs and would not be afraid to inform me what I needed to know from within their sphere, whether it was good news or bad news. I would need to cultivate two-way trust.

Fortunately, I was blessed with excellent people working for me at the Accession and Training Schools. Each day presented new opportunities as well as new challenges, and together we were able to maximize those opportunities and meet those challenges.

My typical day at AFOATS would begin about 6:30 a.m. There was always something going on in the Officer Training School, which I lived close to on the base. The OTS commander might say, "Sir, we're doing a fun run tomorrow, can you come out?" Or they would ask me to address a group of incoming OTS students, or to speak at graduation.

I have to smile when I remember some of the comments that I would receive from the new officer candidates, especially those who had entered the Air Force as enlisted men and had served several years in the military already. "Sir, I don't understand why we have to spend the same amount of time in OTS as someone who is brand new to the Air Force coming out of college," an OTS student would tell me, after respectfully seeking a one-on-one meeting. "Yes, you have experience being in the military," I would say. "But you were an enlisted man; you've never spent a day in your life as an officer. The objective of this program is to teach you to be an officer, and that is very different. There are many things about being an officer that you never learned as an enlisted airman. I can respect and even empathize with your position, having been there myself, but the objective here is what we are trying to achieve and you need to be all-in with that objective." And then I would watch that person relax and sit back in his chair. It was gratifying to apply what I had learned during my training to become an officer to help steer those facing the same transition now.

It was also rewarding to witness the positive results of these programs over the course of many years afterward. The people who served in our center had gone on to make valuable contributions in shaping the military careers and the lives of hundreds of men and women every day.

As well as my natural connection to Officer Training School, I felt a deep resonance with the mission of the college and high school ROTC programs. Sometimes we encountered a sentiment that was fairly common then: Junior ROTC was a recruiting program for the military. Nothing could be further from the truth. Rather than Junior ROTC functioning in high schools as a military recruiting outreach, it's actually a citizenship program that benefits society. We had students in our Junior ROTC programs that never entered the military, because of physical or medical issues or their own personal choice. But each and every one of them who participated in the Junior ROTC program had learned a great deal about becoming a good citizen, and they came away with a strong sentiment of support for our nation's Department of Defense and the military. When given the opportunity to speak to groups of parents of Junior ROTC cadets I would say, "You know, some of your students are going to be Congressmen or Congresswomen someday. Some of them will become leaders in corporate America, or make vital contributions to society. If they carry an understanding and respect for the military, that will benefit the military and our nation." The parents clearly resonated with this message.

As commander, I also had to face those situations when the news at a daily briefing was not always good. Perhaps it would be a day when the ROTC commander would come in and say, "Sir, we have several cadets who aren't meeting academic standards and we've got to decide if we're going to let them stay in the ROTC program and keep them on scholarship or not." Those could be tough calls, especially if the under-performing student came from an environment without the best educational or social opportunities. Sometimes, if a struggling student showed potential, I would conclude that he might merit another chance. Other times the best decision was to let someone go. Every individual merited our full consideration as leaders. Sometimes we would be contacted by parents pleading their child's case, explaining how their son or daughter just had one bad semester and that they couldn't afford to stay in school without the scholarship that came with ROTC participation. No matter how we would rule in a situation like that, I never took a parent's emotional reaction lightly. That parent had entrusted their son or daughter to us.

In other situations, a student in the Air Force ROTC program might be on the cusp of being let go because of one incident of misconduct. I would study those situations closely. I understood that we all made mistakes in college and did something dumb. However, if what they did was not degrading to the program, to the Air Force, or to the nation, perhaps that one mistake was not a good enough reason to take him out. When a leader of one of my programs would question how we could allow a student to remain in the program after a particular offense, I would say, "Because I believe that this young person can be rehabilitated to be a good officer. And rehabilitation is designed to rehabilitate, not eliminate. It ought to be called execution if you're going to 'kill' people. You don't want to kill those people who deserve a chance to succeed."

I remember a phone call I received once from a parent whose son had done something wrong while an ROTC student at a southern university. "My child had a little bit of a problem and I know you are going to make some sort of recommendation regarding his status," he began. Although I expected him to insist that his son remain in the program, he said, "I know you will do the right thing, and whatever the outcome may be, I'm good with it." I studied the case objectively and concluded that this kid had made one of those mistakes that while unfortunate still pointed to allowing a second chance. That's the decision I made, and that young man went on to fly F-16s while serving the Air Force with great devotion and without further incident.

As a commander, I also had to confront situations in which there were no decisions to be made, no words that could be spoken. That was true the day that I learned that a Junior ROTC cadet was stabbed while wearing the uniform in his high school because of an antimilitary sentiment there. What words could possibly convey the anger and sadness over such a horrific act?

That was one of the lowest days of my life, including all the carnage I witnessed moving body bags in Vietnam. There would be another day on my watch that ranked in the same category. This moment emerged after the April 16, 2007 mass shooting at Virginia Tech University in which thirty-two people were killed and seventeen wounded by one gunman. One of those killed, a senior at the university, was an Air Force ROTC student. As commander of the Air Force Accession and Training Schools, I was asked to represent the Air Force at this cadet's funeral. I will never forget as long as I live and have a sound mind what happened when I presented the flag on behalf of our nation and the U.S. Air Force.

"I gave my child to this university and to the Air Force to make him an officer, and you're giving him back to me dead."

Those were the words spoken by a parent of the cadet. I understood that in that moment, I was serving as the target of opportunity for this grieving parent. I just shook my head in empathy and remained silent. There were no words that I could have said that could possibly have soothed this parent's pain.

Those memories have stuck with me, along with the privilege of witnessing newly commissioned officers as they graduated from OTS. Our program would usher more than 500 new officers into the officer ranks every year. I would proudly observe them, with the hope that many would go on to serve ten, twenty or even thirty years as an Air Force officer.

By early spring of 2008 I had been serving as commander of the Air Force Officer Accession and Training Schools for about fifteen months. I had been pinned as Major General on November 2, 2007. I was feeling very much at home and gratified to see the difference that we were able to make in my first command. But as every high-ranking officer knows, you never want to get too comfortable in any one assignment. You never know when the call may come that will take you somewhere else.

My executive and I were driving back from San Angelo, Texas, where we had visited one of our schools, heading for San Antonio and then a flight back to Montgomery. The call came from my three-star boss. This time the message was to inform me of where the Air Force needed me next.

"Al, we're going to send you to the Second Air Force," he said. "You will be the commander there."

"I understand, and I welcome this opportunity," I said. "When do I report to Keesler?" I knew that the Second Air Force was headquartered at Keesler Air Force Base in Biloxi, Mississippi.

"We'll give you more information when you get back to Maxwell," he said.

Back at the base, this boss walked over to my home from his own home just two houses away.

"Being the commander of the Second Air Force will be a great opportunity for you," he said. "We'll need you there in two weeks."

As soon as our meeting ended, I began packing. I was not questioned about whether this new assignment would be something I would want to do, although in this case it absolutely was a tremendous opportunity. In fact, I became the first officer in the history of our finance community to command a numbered Air Force. It was a great honor. But had it been an assignment with far less appeal, it would not have mattered. As a high-ranking Air Force officer you simply understand that you go where you are needed.

Some people may assume that once you climb higher in the chain of command as an officer, you naturally have more input and choice in what you do and where you do it. Ironically, you actually have more input on the lower levels. As a Lieutenant or a Captain, you might get a call from the assignments officer at the personnel center. This would typically be a Major or a Lieutenant Colonel. He or she would talk to you about what they're looking at, about what your next assignment was likely to be, and then you would have an opportunity to respond. Before a final decision was reached, there would be a conversation—a real dialogue. On the senior levels, there is no reason for dialogue. You are a servant leader and ready for what the Air Force needs you to do. They don't mention this, but there is an understanding that if you don't want to go along with the plan, there is what was called a "seven-day op." That means that within seven days after receiving your assignment, you could choose to refuse it. If you did so, sixty days later you would be retired—off the rolls. So you have an option, but it's not a viable one.

This approach is totally different from what any of us would expect in the private sector, where highly accomplished leaders with an excellent track record usually have their pick of multiple places to work at any given time. But as Air Force officers, we all understand the situation. We accept it because it's a basic part of being a servant who has agreed to serve our nation. By the way, there's a major difference between being in service and being a *servant*. Service is simply working in the job that you are assigned to perform, but being a servant means you are willing to go and serve wherever you are called upon to do so as a servant of the nation. So everybody that's a servant is also serving, but not everyone that is serving is a servant. One category is about the job, the other is about an attitude. I always embraced the role of being a servant.

Once again, I would be taking the reins of a huge operation. The Second Air Force is responsible for conducting basic and technical training except pilot training for active duty, guard and reserve Air Force members. Consider the numbers involved. During that time, about 35,000 men and women would go through basic training, which was still held at Lackland Air Force Base, and another 25,000 airmen would engage in technical training, learning in some 2,500 courses.

Operations under the wing of the Second Force extended far and wide geographically. Sheppard Air Force Base in Wichita Falls, Texas was entirely under the domain of the Second Air Force with its maintenance training and civil engineer training. At Goodfellow Air Force Base in San Angelo, Texas, the Second Air Force commanded fire protection training and intelligence training, not only for the Air Force but for the entire Department of Defense. Lackland hosted not just basic training but other specialized training under the Second Air Force, including dog training for the Department of Defense, the FBI and other agencies that utilized highly trained dogs to perform functions such as sniffing for drugs or weapons. Enlisted airmen in space and missile training at Vandenberg Air Force Base in California also were under the domain of the Second Air Force. And back at Keesler Air Force Base, the main home of the Second Air Force, technical training was conducted in communications, finance, special operations and other areas.

So, not only did we cover a lot of ground geographically, we also had a lot of moving parts. When I reported for this assignment, I understood that my primary mission would be to pull all the parts together and maintain a cohesive command. As commander, my first task was to set up a commander's call of all my leaders within my first few hours at Keesler. We discussed the mission of the Second Air Force, going through all the objectives and what we were trying to achieve as a unit, and what each of them were responsible for as commanders. I explained how I operated as a leader, what my primary leadership values were, and how I would relate to those under my command.

My goal in this initial meeting was to establish a strong rapport right up front with my leaders so that they would know who I was, where I was coming from, what they could expect from me and how I would deal with them. On that last reference, I aimed for a simple and direct message that began this way:

"You're the commander; I don't know your job. I trust you and will continue to trust you until you give me reason not to trust you. Then I may have to call you, look you in the eye and say, 'I like you as a person but there has been a loss of confidence and I need to replace you.' I do not expect that to happen. So go do your job, and I will do whatever I can to provide what you need to do it well. I will come out and see what you're doing, and I want you to come see me."

Within that message, it was especially important to them that I acknowledged that I did not know their job. After all, I was still primarily a resourcing professional, although I had just commanded the Accession and Training Schools. I had to acknowledge that to them, and I had to acknowledge it to myself. As a commander, if you act like you know something about their operation and they can see that you really don't know, they will sometimes play games with you. And I wasn't about playing games. We were involved with serious business, the nation's business. So I had to tell them up front that there was much I didn't know but that I was going to learn everything I could about what they were doing and be as clear as possible about what I was responsible for and what they were responsible for. I concluded my opening talk by saying, "I depend on you to take care of what you need to do, I'll do what I can to help you, and we'll both be successful and accomplish the mission."

A typical day commanding the Second Air Force looked a lot different from the typical day at the Accession and Training

Schools, mostly because I probably spent more time at the other locations of our command than I did at Keesler. When I was on base, however, we would usually start off with an ops briefing to go over what had taken place overnight. The purpose of this meeting would be to get me up to speed if there had been any abnormalities in any of the wings we covered that we would be dealing with that day. From there, I would receive an update on the various trainings: how many students we had in school, how many eliminations we had the previous day or previous week, how many we were bringing into training, the current status of the instructor base, how we were doing with instructors for training. Much of the focus would usually center on basic training at Lackland. We would cover how many students we had in training and how many were on medical waivers, as well as reviewing any recent accidents or incidents. I was always eager to know how many airmen would be graduating that week. The graduation ceremony was held every Friday morning at nine o'clock, fifty weeks a year, with anywhere between 400 and 1,000 men and women entering their service in the Air Force.

With so many trainings in so many locations, there was almost always something happening that demanded further review and follow-up. When something happened, the first thing I wanted to know was whether we were we doing everything that we were supposed to do. Had we determined whether one or more of the instructors were at fault? Was there a safety issue? What next steps were called for and how would they be taken?

Regardless of what was happening on any particular day in any of the wings, I always tried to keep my focus on our airmen. How were they doing? What was being done to give them very opportunity to achieve success in the Air Force? Early in my command I was disappointed to learn that the MTI (Military Training

Instructor) force was only about fifty-eight percent manned. By the time I left the command in September 2009, we had increased the force to about ninety percent. That was something that we all could take great pride in. In my home today I still have the blue instructor hat that I received from the MTI training corps as a tribute for my contributions.

Of all the functions of my command, none were more satisfying than to be at Lackland to witness that Friday morning graduation from basic training. Sometimes I was called upon to serve as the reviewing officer, which was a major honor, but even if I was only there in attendance I would be moved by the sight of hundreds of airmen being sworn into active duty. As I would look out at them all, I would wonder who among them might serve for as long as thirty years. There was so much potential.

I probably had hundreds of parents of airmen approach me on that special day. They would want me to know how they felt about what they saw in their child through this experience. "It's amazing what you guys can do with these kids in just eight weeks," they would say. "We sent you our child and now you have made a man or a woman out of him (or her)."

"Well, that's what we do," I would explain. "And now we want that man or woman to defend this nation, to carry the right attitude in whatever work they are asked to do, and to truly become servants."

8

THE *REAL* OBJECTIVE

THROUGH ALL MY YEARS and many assignments as an officer, my command philosophy never changed. I kept it clear and simple:

1. Do the best that you can do, and always do what is right. No matter where you are, how high a ranking you have achieved, or how much responsibility has been entrusted to you, your integrity can never be compromised.

2. Take care of your people. Your people are your most valuable asset and you must take care of every single one of them, even those who struggle and make mistakes. If you *do* take care of your people they will take care of you, and if you *don't* take care of your people they will take care of you...in a bad way.

3. Leave your assignment in a better state than you found it in.

I took that second guiding belief a step further. From early on in my career as an officer in the Air Force, I always believed that my number one objective was not just to take care of my people but to help those I was responsible for to reach their full potential. It wasn't about me—never was, never will be. My approach every day was to provide the men and women around me the opportunity to achieve the greatest possible success and satisfaction in their military careers and beyond. No matter where I was serving or in what capacity, I always welcomed any and all opportunities to encourage, to mentor, to guide or to inspire those who needed such support and were receptive to what I could offer.

That's the approach that I benefitted from in my own career. I had so many superior officers who were willing to encourage, guide and mentor me, as well as to select me for rewarding and meaningful assignments. Their commitment to help me realize my fullest potential was instrumental in enabling me to navigate a military career that lasted forty-six years and propelled me all the way to the rank of Major General.

I remember a comment made to me by one of the Generals who helped guide me to greater heights. "Al, do you know who makes Generals?" he asked me. "I think so, sir," I responded. He nodded his head and continued, "Well, in case you were still wondering, let me tell you. Generals make Generals." I rose as high as I did because others who knew me and my work believed in me and were willing to place me in positions of greater and greater responsibility. And whenever I needed their support or counsel, they were always right there to deliver it. I tried to shape my leadership around the same mindset.

Certainly I had expanded opportunities to encourage and support others in my commands of the Air Force Officer Accession and Training Schools and the Second Air Force. Then, in my final assignment at the Pentagon as Deputy Assistant Secretary for Budget, I found myself leading a team of 160 military, civilian and contractor professionals who worked directly for me, as well as thousands of others in the financial community around the world involved with our mission. It was a call from the Air Force Chief of Staff that opened the door to this assignment. I was responsible for a total budget of $170 billion, including $119 billion that came directly to the Air Force as well as other funds we budgeted for that were parceled out to other organizations. Those who worked for me helped me formulate, justify and defend our budget on Capitol Hill.

We worked hard and took our responsibility seriously, and I always held onto the same perspective that I had carried with me from my first days as an officer back in 1979: each individual serving with me had been entrusted to us by their parents to lead, to train and to help do the business of our great nation. Our troops are not objects and they're not social security numbers; they are people. They deserve first and foremost to be treated with respect and dignity at all times, whether that is when they perform at their best or on those occasions when they may make mistakes. We all make blunders in our work and in our lives. We all do things we regret. As officers and leaders, it is our mission to guide them in good times and harder times, always with that goal of helping them fulfill their greatest potential. I also believe that all of us as military leaders have a responsibility to do our best to make sure that we deliver these young men and women back to their families. Bad things will happen sometimes, but we ought not to have an environment that allows bad things that happen that shouldn't happen.

Supporting and encouraging those who served with me took on many forms. Sometimes it was just a matter of showing up to remind them I was there, that I cared about them as people. Back around 2000, when I was serving as Director of Budget Programs in an earlier assignment at the Pentagon, I was leading a group that had worked twenty-four hours straight in preparing for a budget to go through senior leadership and the Air Force Council before being taken on to Capitol Hill. Although this group had done their best work, we were told that we needed to make some corrections. I was a Colonel at the time, and it was suggested to me by a General involved in the mission that I should collect $5 each from the troops to buy pizza and then keep them around for as long as it would take for them to execute the desired changes. Well, this plan ran counter to my basic command philosophy.

"First of all, I will buy the pizza for my people," I explained. "Second, if you want to keep someone extra time, keep me. The troops need to go home." After eating the pizza I brought in and working for less than an hour, we all got to go home.

Another story from that same assignment was described by my friend Joseph Ward, who twice served with me during his own highly successful career. As Joe remembers it, I had just come out of a meeting with a two-star General at 1700 hours one afternoon when I handed Joe the ambitious task of completing 30 primary slides and 300 backup slides for a budget briefing first thing the next morning. "Can you accomplish this task by the deadline?" I asked. Joe responded that he could and he would, as long as he had another officer to assist him and they could work through the night without interruption. I agreed and expressed my gratitude. Joe relates what happened next.

"Colonel Flowers left the office late that evening, but a couple of hours later, right around midnight, he arrived back, still in uniform, carrying two large bags of Kentucky Fried Chicken with all the fixings. That was the best chicken dinner I ever had, and after that delivery Colonel Flowers never left the office. All night long he made sure the coffee pot stayed full and just kept speaking words of encouragement to us. He always took care of everyone around him."

The way I remember that night, I was just doing my job. Joe and his fellow officer were the ones doing the real work, meeting the challenge handed to them with grace and commitment. They deserved my full backing, in whatever way I could demonstrate it.

That was the same spirit with which I approached a difficult situation during my command of the Second Air Force. Due to a government stalemate in Washington, the budget year was about to end with no agreement on a one-year appropriation funding. In other words, there appeared to be a very real possibility that our troops were not going to be paid.

I knew that I had to stand up for my people. I promised our senior NCOs (non-commissioned officers) that everybody was going to get paid, even if I had to personally work with the credit unions to obtain loans to keep their paychecks coming. I had a firm plan in place to ensure that everyone, especially those young airmen that couldn't afford to not be paid, would have their pay coming their way on time. As fate would have it, the government, five minutes before midnight, agreed on a continuing resolution authority so that the funds kept coming. My plan to personally intervene would not need to be implemented.

Years later I ran into a Chief Master Sergeant who had since retired. He immediately reminded me of that moment of uncertainty in 2007.

"When the troops were not going to get paid, and everybody else was complaining and whining about what was going to happen and how bad it would be, you just stood up and said, 'It's not going to happen. I'm going to find a way for you folks to get paid.'

We were all so grateful for what you did. You know, you're an American hero," he said.

"I am not," I replied. "I'm just an individual that tried to do my best and take care of the troops. If the situation repeated itself, I would do the same thing again."

Both before and after my retirement from the Air Force, I've been gratified to hear from many airmen whom I guided, encouraged or mentored as individuals. I don't usually talk about those moments of appreciation or validation because I have never wanted other folks to think I was bragging on myself or my leadership abilities. But in the interest of reminding current or potential leaders of the kind of difference they can make in the lives of others, I will offer a few examples.

The first relates to Thomas Carter, an officer who came to the Pentagon to be interviewed for a position while I was Director of Budget Programs. At that time, if you were being considered for a position on our staff you had to work your way through all the directors during the interview process. I happened to be the last stop for this candidate.

"Tell me what you want to be doing ten years from now," I advised Major Carter.

"I want to be a professor at a historical black college or university teaching ROTC," he responded.

"Okay, I understand why you would say that. But if you interview with anybody else, don't tell them that," I said.

"Sir, why not?" he asked with a bewildered look.

"Because you're better than that," I said calmly. "In ten years you could be a Colonel in the Air Force leading some major command budget, or serving as a chief financial officer. If you come work for me, that will be my objective for you. And I'm going to tell you right now, I am going to hire you and you're coming to Washington to work in this office."

"Wow, I've never had anybody take an interest in me like that and tell me that his objective is for me to have a better career than what I imagined could be possible," he said.

So Thomas Carter did come to work for me, he applied great effort in his assignment in the Pentagon and he continued to advance, eventually retiring as the chief financial officer for a large agency. When I saw him in San Antonio recently, he told me that I probably didn't realize the impact that I had on his career and his life. "Well, I hope the impact was positive," I said with a grin.

Sometimes I would find myself dealing with an airman in some situation that reminded me of my own experience. That was the case one day when I was contacted by a General while I was commanding the Second Air Force. "Officer Flowers, I have a problem," he said. He went on to explain that his relative, who had just completed basic training at Lackland as a six-year enlistee, did not receive the career field he requested. He happened to want to work in finance, but instead he was being placed with the security forces. Well, after doing some checking I discovered that while the Air Force had a need for security personnel, this relative had scored extremely well on the ASVAB (Armed Services Vocational Aptitude Battery) and we tried to maintain a commitment to give six-year enlistees with excellent scores their first or second career choice. I remembered the experience of seeking a position in finance when I was starting out after basic training and instead receiving more than one assignment in cargo handling. However, my first responsibility here was to do the right thing. If there had been some compelling reason to deny this airman his choice, the fact that he was a General's relative would not be reason enough to reverse the decision.

So I called the classifiers that worked for me and asked them to check into the case. "We made a mistake here, boss," one of them reported later. "This airman scored in the ninetieth percentile on his ASVAB and as a six-year enlistee we should have tried to give him his first or second choice. His first choice is finance and we need people there, too. We will reclassify him and put him into that career field."

A few months later I was on Keesler Air Force Base, headquarters of the Second Air Force, when I saw a young man walking down the street. I wondered why he was out of class walking around alone, so I pulled up and looked at the name tag.

"You wouldn't by any chance have a relative who's a retired Air Force two-star?" I asked. Looking a bit uneasy he responded, "Yes, sir." When I told him to get in my car and asked him why he was out by himself at that time, he told me he was sick and was walking to the hospital. "Then I'll take you there right now," I said, and on the way there he told me he was going through finance technical school. So I kept track of him and at last account he was doing fine. I was pleased that I had been able to assist this airman, just by doing the right thing.

Even before I became an officer I tried to provide encouragement to those who may have needed a little boost. Back in the 1970s, when I was serving as an accounting specialist at Charleston Air Force Base while working on my bachelor's degree from Southern Illinois University, I was on the golf course one day with a fellow named George. He was a Master Sergeant (E-7) at the time with more than fifteen years of service. He told me that he was thinking about retiring from the Air Force so that he could go to college and obtain a position to improve his situation. I reminded him that I was enrolled at the Southern Illinois extension program, working on my college degree right there on the base.

"Man, where do you find the time to go to school full-time on evenings and weekends and still do your work here?" he asked.

"I don't find the time. I make the time," I explained. "We all have the same twenty-four hours a day; it's just a matter of how we use it. Why don't you join me? If you get your degree while you're still in the Air Force, you might retire as an E-8 (Senior Master Sergeant) or even an E-9 (Chief Master Sergeant)."

He thought about this for awhile and finally decided to enroll in the Southern Illinois University program. He found the time to do his job and keep up with his studies in class, and he graduated. And by the time he retired from the Air Force, after thirty years of distinguished service, George had earned two more promotions to reach the rank of Chief Master Sergeant.

When I see him during my return visits to North Carolina these days, he tells me, "Al, do you remember when you suggested that I follow you in that SIU program at Charleston? If it hadn't been for you I would have probably retired as a Master Sergeant. I owe that to you."

"You don't owe anything to me," I insisted. "I didn't do your work for you. You did it. The only thing I did was suggest that you go to school and see what the outcome would be."

I remember another example where an airman needed encouragement regarding his education and future career. Glenn was an enlisted man working with me as an administrative specialist in 1993. He had entered the Air Force after being raised on one of the islands and was a Technical Sergeant (E6) when he approached me seeking guidance.

"Sir, how do I become an officer and develop a successful career as an officer?" he asked me one day.

"Well, in order to be an officer you have to have a college degree. I'm pleased to see that you've already begun working on that," I began. "So you need to finish your degree and then begin the application process for OTS, which includes getting letters of recommendation from supervisors. Then you wait and see what happens."

When Glenn asked me if I would write a letter of recommendation for him, I was happy to do so. Unfortunately, his application was denied, which is something I could certainly appreciate after being rejected three times before an officer intervened and helped me get my foot in the door. Like me, Glenn just applied again. I wrote another letter on his behalf, and this time he was accepted. After successfully completing Officer Training School, he began a financial career that carried him all the way to the rank of Major. Whenever he sees me, he is quick to give me credit, and I am just as quick to say, "All I did was explain what the possibilities could be. You made it come true for yourself. You got where you did because of you."

Not everyone that I have had the opportunity to guide or mentor wore the uniform of the U.S. Air Force. While I was commanding the Accession and Training Schools at Maxwell Air Force Base, my personnel officer was a very bright civilian woman. She was struggling. She really hoped to further her education and earn a promotion but was working full-time while raising two teenagers and just couldn't see how to fit everything on her plate.

"I just can't do it. It's too much," she said of her college studies.

"It's only too much if you let it be too much," I assured her. "I would recommend that you think more about your priorities. I'm sure that for you, family is first—always. Then I expect you to continue to perform as well as you do in your job here, which you do very well. After that, maybe you need to figure out how you can strike a balance where you can do school, too, so that you can earn that degree to open up the opportunities for promotion that you want for yourself and to help your family."

She thought about this for a moment and then smiled. "Okay, it will take me a long time to finish college, but I'm going to try," she said.

Well, it didn't take her nearly as long as she anticipated. With commitment and determination, and her priorities clear, she earned her bachelor's degree and was well on her way to a master's the last time I spoke to her. "You pushed me when I needed a push," she said, to which I replied, "I didn't push you anywhere. You asked me how you could do it and you pushed yourself."

Kerry was already an Air Force officer in 2001 while serving in the Air Education and Training Command at Randolph Air Force Base in San Antonio. Kerry had been a command post officer but decided to retrain into budget. The only problem was that he didn't know much about budget and lacked experience in that arena. Still, when I met him after being assigned as Comptroller for Air Education and Training, I liked him enough to select him to be my second executive. That's when he informed me that he was so discouraged that he was considering leaving the Air Force.

"Why are you even thinking that?" I asked. "Listen, when you're serving in the military there are going to be a lot of bumps in the road. Just because you hit a pothole, you don't go trade your car in. And I'll tell you, this is not even a pothole. You're in a career field now where folks will do everything they can to help you be as successful as you possibly can be and reach your greatest potential. So here you are with me, as my exec, and we're going to get started on this journey right now."

I taught him everything that I knew, and Kerry was extremely attentive. I gave him an open invitation to ask me why I made any decision that I reached, or how I viewed any situation, and he took me up on it. He asked questions all the time. I remember one time we were sitting together when I had to deny a recommendation by one of our directors and advise him to go in a different direction. Kerry, who seemed to believe that the director was on solid ground in his proposal, wanted to know why.

"It is true that the director had thought through many of the details of what he was about to do, but he had not given enough consideration to the strategic view, how it would impact others, or how it fit with the commander or the vice commander's point of view," I explained. "Kerry, this is what they pay me for. I understand what folks above me and those above them are thinking, and how to make a decision that's in the best interest of the entire command."

Kerry eagerly soaked in all of my experience and advice, and he learned quickly. Before I left Randolph he had advanced to my primary executive, and he was just getting started. He went on to become a Comptroller, at the rank of Major, and is now a Colonel serving as Director of Legislative affairs for Air Force Budget Head-quarters. In that assignment, he interacts with Congress on behalf of the Air Force and the Appropriations Committee. He has taken several big steps since I worked with him, and I have often con-sulted with him or his superiors along the way. His wife often jokes with Kerry that when he has a question about some new possibility being floated in front of him, he should "go check with your father." She is referring to me, and while it's certainly rewarding to be regarded in that light, it truly has been my pleasure to mentor this talented officer and watch him achieve the success he has enjoyed.

Kerry was just one of many examples of the cream rising to the top. I've had several executive officers work for me during my career, and they have all done extremely well, just as I knew they would. I selected them to be my executive officers because of their attitude, as well as their abilities. It didn't matter if they were white, black, Hispanic or some other ethnicity. They cared about perform-ing at their best and they worked to achieve their full potential.

High School grad, 1965

Airman 3C Flowers, December '65

Airman 2nd Class Flowers, Grand Forks, ND '66

Officer Training School graduation,
December '78

Then-Captain Alfred Flowers at the
Pentagon, November '85

Lieutenant Colonel Alfred K.
Flowers, April 29, '92

Commissioning Al Jr., '98

Colonel Flowers, '98

Al Jr. Wedding Day, August '98

Mama Lucy who raised me (sitting), my mother Annie, Uncle Buddy, me and Ida.

2011

Al Jr. presents U. S. flag at retirement ceremony

Al Jr., Al III, and Ayden presenting gift at retirement dinner

Being informed of receiving the Order of the Sword by CMSgt. Cody at Pentagon, November 2011

At Air Force Memorial, November 2011

Air Force Memorial, November 2011

Gen. Flowers and Buddy at church, 2015

That list includes Darnell, my last executive officer when I was on active duty in the Pentagon. Darnell was very bright, and I'm not ashamed to admit that he was really a better budget officer than I ever was. Yet, as talented as he was, Darnell had not been promoted at the pace he probably deserved and was struggling with what to do next after working for me as a Lieutenant Colonel. Retirement from the Air Force was an active consideration.

"You know, with your record, your performance and your demeanor, you look like a recruiting poster board for the Air Force," I told him one day. "I think you should apply to work at the White House military office. We always have one budget officer working over there, and I have had a role in a couple of our people landing those positions. Why don't you apply?"

I had my eye on him for this possibility for awhile. As well as his excellent performance, he was slim and trim, no fat anywhere on him, and just looked good in uniform: the epitome of the ideal professional officer.

"The White House? Oh, sir, they would never select me over there," he sighed.

"Well, they won't select you if you don't apply," I responded sternly, and after a little more encouragement he agreed to apply.

"I'll need somebody to write a recommendation," he pointed out.

"You've got somebody—same person that recommended that you apply," I smiled. "Don't worry about a recommendation. That's in my job jar."

So I wrote that letter, Darnell aced his interviews and he landed that position in the White House military office. I was definitely proud of Darnell and I have to say that I greatly enjoyed my little "reward" as well. He invited my wife and I, along with my sister, my niece and her two children, to lunch in the West Wing of the

White House! We did not see President Obama but we got the full treatment: reserved table, private menu with your name on it, the works. I would never have dreamed that someday I would be having lunch in the White House, and I had that opportunity simply because I helped one of my dedicated officers reach his fullest potential. In fact, after leaving the White House Darnell has continued to advance in his career. And he still looks like a recruiting poster for the Air Force.

Over the years, some people have suggested that maybe I've been a little bit foolish to spend so much time taking care of other people when I could be spending more of that time taking care of myself. I just say that I'm simply doing my job. Besides, the rewards are immeasurable. I gain great satisfaction from guiding and encouraging other people, and they're apt to be receptive when they know that you're being genuine, that you really do care about them as people.

This emphasis in my leadership approach also goes back to being raised by my two loving and supportive grandparents, and the village that supported and nurtured me. With the values that were instilled in me growing up, it's natural that I'd feel good about recognizing and acting upon a belief that I can say or do something that might change someone's life and the way they feel about a situation. I'm not as eager to offer my input to those folks who think they've got it all figured out. The way I see it, if you've got it all figured out already you don't need me to waste my energy on you because you're wasting your own. Expending my energy trying to help people like that is tiring. I'd much rather deal with someone that's genuine about needing help or direction, and appreciative of receiving it.

I also try hard not to kid myself that it's only someone like me, with all my years of experience and whatever I happened to have achieved, who has the ability to mentor someone. There are many times in my life, especially since my retirement, when I have turned to someone much younger than me and said, "Hey, I need some mentoring here. Can you help me?" If they say, "Oh, sir, you don't need my help" I have to assure them that I don't have it all figured out. "I do need your mentoring because you know what you're doing in this situation and I'm trying to learn. The fact that you may be thirty years younger than me doesn't make one bit of difference," I assure them.

The reality is that we all learn from each other. Our experiences and our strengths are different, but when we are willing to genuinely share what we have learned with those around us, no matter who they are, we all have a greater opportunity to shine.

THE NEW MISSION

MY RETIREMENT from the Air Force at the start of 2012 marked the end of my career as the longest-serving airman in Air Force history, but it did not signal the end of my commitment to make a difference in the lives of others. I simply approached that goal through a new mission: giving back for all that I had received in my forty-six years as an enlisted man and officer in the U.S. Air Force.

In retirement, I would seek out and commit to new opportunities to assist men and women currently serving in the military, military veterans and their families, young people striving to overcome hardships and challenges so that they could achieve success in the world, and other groups and causes that I believed were worthy of my time and energy.

My nature hadn't changed at all. I still had that same desire to take care of other people. I just had to find different environments and new ways to make that happen. The landscape would include volunteering to serve on boards of organizations whose missions were aligned with mine and accepting some of the many speaking invitations extended to me by schools, businesses and organizations inside and outside the military. Perhaps there would be businesses that would call me with job offers, even though I was "retired."

At the same time, I also had to face a humbling reality. After taking off my Air Force Major General uniform, leaving behind the bustling offices of the Pentagon and stepping away from the insulated world of large military bases all over the country, I was going to be a fish out of water.

I remember my first post-retirement day. I was sitting in my office at home, just quietly thinking about my years of service as reflected by the various awards, citations and photos all around me, when my wife Ida walked in.

"Well, look at you," she began in her affectionate but directly honest manner. "You have no personal aide, no staff of assistants, just me and your own personal life. Guess you're going to have to learn to do things in a different way."

She had that right. I had grown very accustomed to having five people in my office doing assorted tasks for me, or preparing something to submit for my review. Now I was just sitting around alone staring at four walls. I was used to having assistance going wherever I needed or wanted to go. Now I had two cars of my own out front, and I was holding the keys, but I had no one to assist me with getting anywhere. Life certainly was going to be a lot different!

Through discussions with many colleagues in similar situations, I have learned more about how the jolting changes coming out of a long military career are not just superficial. Living on a military base, you get used to a strong community of mutual support and understanding. In a way, however, you are segregated from the world. Then, when you take off the uniform and spend all your time in that outside world, you may discover that folks don't care as much about you or your service as you *thought* they did. You find yourself adapting to an exaggerated sense of importance. For those who leave the military and enter the civilian work world, reality takes the form of being plopped into a very different work culture, where making money, not service, is the primary objective. Moral, legal or ethical questions may emerge. In the Air Force and the other services you do whatever it takes, including dying for your fellow airmen. In the corporate world, it may be difficult to find someone willing to die for you.

I believe that while we do an excellent job of training airmen how to enter the Air Force through basic training, we do not do nearly as effective a job at training them how to leave. Whether airmen serve four years or twenty-four years, they need to be better prepared for taking that big step out of the military into non-military life. That's one more cause that I may be investing my time in.

I should emphasize that I welcomed most of what was put in front of me in my post-military transition. One welcome change was being free to do more with my wife and family. I had always held so much gratitude for what Ida had done to support and enable me to maintain my commitment to the Air Force. She had been with me all the way since we met and married in 1969, through at least twenty-two moves necessitated by rapidly-changing assignments. I could never have done what I did without her.

When the moves started coming every two years or less, there were a few moments when she pulled me aside to say, "Sweetheart, you know these moves aren't getting any easier" as she hinted at the idea of retirement. I would just respond, "If you're getting to the end of your rope, you need to tie a knot and hang on, because we're going to go awhile longer." And each time she would agree to keep on dealing with the packing and unpacking, and the adjustments to living in new places, around people she didn't know.

If I had any regret at all about my years of military service it would be working all those sixty, seventy or eighty-hour weeks on many of those demanding assignments. I had made a conscious decision to try to make as much of a contribution as I possibly could as a servant in the Air Force, and I believed that I could adequately balance work and family life—that I could do it all. Well, the reality is that you can't do it all. Something suffers when you try. There were many occasions when I probably should have been at home, or attending something at school with our son, or venturing out to a cultural event with my family when I was zeroed in on what needed to be done in the office instead.

If I could do it all over again, I would probably choose to take the same route but travel a different road. In other words, I would have figured out some way to spend more time with my family. Our train didn't crash, unlike many other marriages and family relationships I watched come apart with some of my colleagues, but we did hit a few bumps. And the way I look at it, when you lose a day of quality time with your family today, even if you have a day together tomorrow there is still that day you lost yesterday. You can't ever regain it. Lost time is lost time.

At least now I had opportunities to make different kinds of choices. Ida and I enjoyed an extended anniversary trip to Tampa. We made more frequent visits back to North Carolina, spending more time with family and old friends and making quick getaways to the shore so my wife could get her ocean fix. When we were approaching our first Christmas in retirement, I was putting up some decorations for the tree when I missed a step and fell, result-

ing in a detached patella tendon of my left knee. After surgery a
few days before Christmas, Ida and I spent the entire holiday at
home in our PJs, just chit-chatting and watching movies on TV.
That was a welcome change from the rushed routine we had been
locked into for so many years.

I also had a greater opportunity to sit back and appreciate the
Air Force career of our son Al Junior. During my last assignment
at the Pentagon, he was able to visit us frequently while stationed
nearby in Virginia. In retirement, we had more flexibility to choose
when to visit him or to open our home to him and his family. As I
write this, Al Junior has risen to the rank of Colonel and is serving
in Germany. Believe it or not, it was not predestined that he would
follow in my military officer footsteps. It was almost the opposite.
After he had played college basketball at Rider University and was
working on a Master's in Hospital Administration there, I fully
expected him to follow the much more lucrative path of working
in the civilian ranks. As my son explains it, he had other ideas:

> *"When my dad was stationed at Moody Air Force Base
> while I was growing up, I would look up at those F-4 Phantom
> jets and say to myself, 'I wonder if I can do that someday?' I
> attended the Naval Academy prep school, but it just wasn't the
> right time or situation for a military life then. When I was an
> undergraduate at Rider I was in Air Force ROTC for awhile,
> but I left that. Then, when I was moving toward a career in
> hospital administration, I realized that I really wanted to be
> like my dad.*
>
> *I was a proud military brat, and growing up that way built
> the fiber of who I am. I value the tight bonds and personal
> relationships that are formed in the military community, and I
> liked the idea of being part of a greater cause and committing*

to the life of a servant leader. But that wasn't the way I had been talking most of the time I was in school, so when I called my dad up and said, 'Can you come up here next week and swear me in as an Air Force officer?' I swear the phone dropped."

That was about right. I knew that Al Junior could make at least twice as much money as a civilian as he would as a newly commissioned Air Force officer, but when he told me what he wanted to do on that day soon before he completed his master's, I just said, "Well, you're your own man. I hope you know what you're doing." I commissioned him at the recruiting office just off the Rider campus and he entered the Air Force as a First Lieutenant because of his advanced degree. Although I would mentor him when asked, I made it a point to have nothing to do with the selection of any of his assignments. He would be making it on his own. And I have been very proud of how he has found his way over the course of almost two decades as an officer. He has done a great deal to make the Air Force our "family business."

In fact, Al Junior met his wife Liza while she was serving as an Air Force nurse—in the same ward of the same military hospital, Wilford Hall Medical Center, where Al Junior was born. They have two teenage sons, and my grandsons seem to be headed in a similar direction. The oldest set a goal to attend the Air Force Academy where he recently attended a summer camp and flew in a Cessna with an instructor. The other has been in the Civil Air Patrol and wants to go to Harvard. I have been telling them that "if you want to stay in the will, you better think military," and it's not exactly a joke. By the way, the oldest boy is Alfred K. Flowers III and the youngest is Ayden Kristopher, the same A.K. initials that I have. As my son and I proudly agree, names mean something.

So does the commitment to keep the military tradition nearby in our daily lives. Ida and I quickly agreed that our primary retirement home would be in San Antonio, partly because the services and climate were favorable but also because San Antonio is "Military City USA." Lackland and Randolph Air Force bases are there, of course, and Fort Sam Houston, a long-time Army base, had joined Lackland and Randolph in Joint Base San Antonio with the Air Force as the supporting service. Also, within the city's medical sphere, SAMMC (San Antonio Military Medical Center) had expanded to become the Defense Department's largest in-patient hospital. The economic impact from the military for the city of San Antonio is more than $40 billion per year.

My wife and I also shared a personal history in San Antonio. It was her position that led us to Lackland back in 1971 for a one-year assignment during which I served as an accounting specialist, and we came back in 1978 when I attended Officer Training School. Then we enjoyed our two years living in the tight-knit community at Randolph when I was Comptroller with the Air Education and Training Command from September 2001 to August 2003, and I visited Lackland frequently while commander of the Second Air Force later. We had once bought land in the city but never developed it. As we prepared to set up our home for retirement, we persevered through the careful house selection process until we finally landed on the forty-third house that we looked at. When you're making the switch from forty-plus years of temporary living quarters to something much more permanent, you want to do it right.

So even if I had to be a fish out water in adjusting to a different kind of day-to-day life, at least I was near some familiar streams. Living in San Antonio also meant maintaining close contact with airmen who served with me at some time or place along the way.

Awhile back I was being prepped for hand surgery in a San Antonio hospital when the young surgeon approached me.

"Do you remember me? I was in Officer Training School class when you were the commander," he said, referring to the time that I was head of the Accession and Training Schools.

"Well, I'm glad that everything went well for you," I smiled, "because I would hate for you to still be angry at me while you were getting ready to do surgery on me."

The same thing happened at a dentist's office, and there's usually a stream of people waiting to come up and shake hands or give me a hug when I'm on one of the bases. When they ask if I remember them, I honestly answer "no" most of the time because I served with thousands of men and women over so many years and just can't remember each of them. I just politely respond, "Good to see that you're doing well. Thank you for your service." I am even approached by those who know me when I visit my son in Germany, or when I travel just about anywhere where the Air Force has a viable presence. Even when these interactions are brief, I always find them gratifying. These are people who often go out of their way to come up to me and acknowledge me for something I did or said that somehow made a difference in their life. It reminds me that while I was still on active duty, I really did fulfill my mission.

As I have mentioned, the only legacy that interested me was to leave behind people of all ages and backgrounds that I had helped lead, train, mentor and educate who were then able to perform equal to or better than I did. When I'm done and they've buried me someplace, I don't want someone to stand up at my funeral and say, "Well, General Flowers served honorably, he did a great job and accomplished some wonderful things, but all that is gone now because he's gone." I would like to believe that someone might say instead, "He served honorably, he did his best every day, and there are hundreds of folks whose lives that he touched that are very successful at what they do, demonstrating outstanding performance and service."

I also appreciated the many tangible honors and accolades that came my way before and after I retired from the Air Force. I keep many of these distinguished honors in my home, including congratulation letters from our five living former presidents—Jimmy Carter, George H.W. Bush, Bill Clinton, George W. Bush, Barack Obama—which I display under a painting of the Tuskegee Airmen, the noted group of African American pilots that served in World War II. That painting stands as a dramatic reminder of the significant contributions of minorities in our military history.

Over the last several decades, the military has been one of the organizations at the forefront of integration and equal opportunity. We've come a long way from the race riots I remember now and then at my first bases in the '60s. If it hadn't been for equal opportunity, I wouldn't have reached the status I was able to achieve. While I served, I watched the steady improvement of racial relations in the military. We all sought to maintain a commitment of simply not tolerating racism in any way, shape or form. When we learned of any kind of racially motivated act or intention, we dealt with it immediately and aggressively. This is how it should be. Now, were there individuals who entered the military with racial bias or issues? Absolutely. The military, after all, is a microcosm of society. Every person who joins the military brings his or her own personality, upbringing, attitudes and beliefs. Many are good at concealing those negative beliefs until they surface in the military. That's when we step in to rectify the situation.

I can't say that I was never the recipient of discriminatory acts or words. I may have been passed over a time or two for a better position where race was a consideration. However, the evidence overwhelmingly points in the opposite direction. As an African American, the longest-serving African American in the Department of Defense when I left the military, I was treated with fairness, justice and deep respect by almost everyone with whom I served. I absolutely was provided many opportunities to succeed.

I will always be grateful for the support of people like Doug Bunger, who was instrumental in my landing excellent assignments during the early phase of my career as an officer. One boss saw something in me as an officer, not as a black officer or a white officer. He had many of both races to choose from to do his work and to mentor as a leader, and he chose me. He happened to have grown up in Arkansas, so he knew what discrimination was. He could have fallen into influences from his past, but he didn't. I never saw him do anything that even teetered on unfairness or discrimination.

I encountered many other examples of those deeply committed to fairness and justice in regards to race in all my years in the military. Yet, the other side did poke its head up now and again. As recently as four or five years ago, I happened to be visiting one of the bases in the South. It was about 11 p.m. when my wife and I arrived at the main gate and I showed the security guard my Air Force ID, identifying me as a Major General. He looked at the ID and then looked closely at me.

"Okay, now where is *your* ID card?" he said finally, obviously implying that I had stolen somebody else's ID because a black man wouldn't have an ID card that said Major General.

"This is my ID," I said firmly. "And if I need to call your boss, the base commander, to help you understand it's mine, I can do that." The base commander at that time happened to be a gentleman who had just finished working for me. The guard's face turned red. Thank God he was a civilian because if he had been in the military he would have been in for a *very* long night.

"Okay," he muttered. "Now let me see your wife's card."

We honored his request and entered the base without further incident. That experience served as a reminder of the deep-seated prejudices that still exist with some people today. I attribute it to a lack of education, where the individual has chosen not to educate him or herself about the wrongness of that kind of behavior.

Fortunately, though, that does not happen often in the military. People of all races are provided opportunities to perform and succeed, although minorities could still benefit from greater representation in the higher officer ranks. I want to believe that efforts are being made to change that picture.

Other honors that I proudly display at home include the blue hat worn by Military Training Instructors and a rope from technical training, gifts linked to my command of the Second Air Force. I also enjoy gazing at the photo of me reviewing the troops at a graduation ceremony from basic training at Lackland. Visitors to my home also notice that I have an actual piece of the Pentagon as a replica of my many years and varied assignments there.

Of all these and many more representations of my career, I have no trouble singling out the one that means the most to me personally. On April 6, 2012, I became the proud recipient of the Air Force Order of the Sword. This particular honor doesn't come from presidents or senators, and it didn't originate from within the office walls of high-ranking officials. Not at all. The Order of the Sword, launched in 1967, was established by the Air Force enlisted force as a means to recognize and honor senior military officers and civilian equivalents. According to the award's description, noncommissioned officers bestow the honor for conspicuous and significant contributions to the welfare and prestige of the Air

Force enlisted force, mission effectiveness and the overall military establishment. I've got a simpler way to explain it. It's a special way for the enlisted corps to say "we care about you because of how much you cared about us." As someone who served more than thirteen years in the Air Force enlisted force before advancing to my career as an officer, I can't think of any higher honor.

The vote is held in secrecy, and I was told that it was unanimous. The award has been bestowed to about 250 individuals, and most recipients have been three-star or four-star Generals. As a two-star, I was unusual. The award ceremony was held at Randolph Air Force Base because I was recognized for my service with Air Education and Training Command, specifically the contributions I was able to make to the enlisted force as Commander of Second Air Force and the Accession and Training Schools. I am one of only eight officers that have been chosen out of their service with the Air Education and Training Command.

I was touched to be chosen for the Order of the Sword, and I was even more touched by the way they presented it. My wife Ida and I were invited to spend the night on the base at Randolph, and we were told to be ready to be picked up for the ceremony at 5 p.m. At the designated hour, a white, horse-drawn carriage steered by a driver with white tux and tie pulled up to Building 110, where we were being billeted. After being formally escorted to our seats in the carriage, the horses started out toward Parr Club, where the ceremony was to be held.

Being transported like that was impressive enough, but there was more. As our procession unfolded on the narrow streets of the base, the sidewalks on both sides of the street were lined with airmen of all ranks, all in uniform and all ready to applaud and salute us as we passed by. Many of those airmen were folks that I recognized, but even those I didn't know personally I still felt instantly connected to. Whatever their rank, there was a pretty good chance I had been there during my own career, and each one was a representation of the men and women whom I had the honor to serve with and try to assist in reaching their full potential.

The two-hour dinner and speaking event inside included my introduction by Chief Master Sergeant James Cody, the Air Education and Training Command Chief who went on to serve as Chief Master Sergeant of the Air Force. "This is the highest level of recognition that the enlisted force can bestow upon anyone," Chief Master Sergeant Cody began. "Without question, what General Flowers has contributed to the enlisted force throughout his career, specifically for us in AETC, as the Second Air Force commander and then as he moved on to be the Air Force financial manager, has certainly furthered their development, furthered their ability to meet the demands and needs of our nation."

With other important members of my family present in the small exclusive audience, I tried to express my overwhelming gratitude and appreciation for all those who contributed to my service and my receiving the Order of the Sword. "I could not make myself successful," I said. "I'm not smart enough, I'm not good enough. It's the men and women that surrounded me that made me as successful as I became. I'm honored that the noncommissioned officers selected me to receive this and I'm humbled by the whole experience. This is as good as it gets."

I have the four-foot long sword presented to me that night, along with an oil painting of Ida and me given to us to commemorate the event, in my home in San Antonio. All these many honors, accolades and awards that I have held onto are important reminders of my career and how I wound up as the longest serving airman in the history of the Air Force and the longest serving African American in any of the military branches. Both of those honors are rich with meaning for me. Being the longest serving airman is special because of how I started at the bottom, worked my way up to Master Sergeant and then, after thirteen and a half years in the enlisted corps, went on to not only become an officer but a senior officer and general officer. What pulls at my heartstring about that is to know that I had the courage and tenacity, as well as the help and assistance from so many people, to be entrusted with several very important positions.

Service is not easy. Nothing about it is guaranteed. Many bright and talented individuals enter the military with the aim of advancing to a high level but don't stay that long, whether because of problems of adaptability, health issues, getting in trouble or some other factor. I endured because others who assessed my performance believed that I was making a difference. I believed that too, because if I had not believed it I would have done something else somewhere along the forty-six year path.

Retiring as the longest serving African American in the history of defense carries major significance for me because of all the contributions that have been made for decades by African Americans that were not always recognized. Whenever I am asked to speak on Martin Luther King Day, I seek not only to honor Dr. King but also to highlight the examples of major contributions made by other African Americans who did not happen to be famous. So many should have been recognized but never were. I am deeply grateful that I gained high recognition for doing what I did as long as I did it, but that recognition is not all about me personally. It's also about being an African American. I just chose black parents, but I embrace the notoriety on behalf of those who didn't receive it.

Going back to my activities in my transition to post-military life, that first year after leaving Washington was also the official "cooling off period" when you can't represent back to the Air

Force or do any business with the Air Force. I elected not to have any relationship with the entire government during that time because the Air Force worked with so many other government entities. I did do some work for non-profits, making sure that they had no involvement at all with the Air Force.

In January 2013, after that hands-off period had expired, I got a call from the president of a certified cyber security, IT and engineering services firm with a home office in San Antonio. "Can you come in and have a chat?" the caller asked. "I would if I could, but I am not able to leave the house right now," I said, explaining about my knee surgery over the holidays. "Then can I come to your home and talk with you there?" he countered. I accepted an offer to serve as a consultant, working with limited hours. A couple of years into my new civilian employment I took on the role of Chief Operating Officer, with an assurance of working only twenty-five hours a week to preserve my new life choices at home. The business has grown rapidly during my time there, and I believe that my name recognition and contacts have been useful. I still hold that COO position today, although I can see the finish line when I will "retire" again. Of course, as I told friends when I got hired, I had failed at retirement once, so we'll see what happens.

Working in a civilian environment, it was important to me that I could still approach leadership with the same priority: taking care of people around me and helping them reach their full potential. In the private sector, I learned from a fresh perspective the importance of creating an environment where your people put their families first. As long as the work gets done, they should have freedom and flexibility to take care of their lives at home. With everything I tried to do in this new kind of professional mission, I was still committed to making a difference.

While I was experiencing civilian work life for the first time as an adult, I also kept up my commitments to many boards. Some related to the needs of San Antonio, where much of the minority-dominated east side of the city lives in poverty, but as time went on more and more of my volunteer hours circled back to the military. That's where my new mission of giving back entered into the equation.

We hear a lot of talk nationally these days about the need to do more for our veterans. There's no question that there is great need in this area. Even after their time of service to our nation ends, veterans continue to do so much to assist society. How often do we see veterans among our police ranks or fire departments, our postal service staff and other entities that serve our communities? Yet many veterans are struggling. I have seen statistics that indicate that one of every four homeless people in our country are veterans, and that nine of ten were honorably discharged. Many suffer from PTSD symptoms. Hundreds of thousands of vets are unemployed or under-employed, with a disproportionate number living below the poverty line.

One organization devoted to the cause of these veterans is the Air Force Aid Society. I've been on the Board of Trustees there for several years and have done whatever I could to boost our program donations and to better utilize the funds to serve veterans. Our CEO learned that we had been providing aid to needy veterans mostly in the form of loans. His thinking was that if you're in financial need and that need is long-term, getting a loan is probably just going to exacerbate the problem. Giving them a loan and then hounding them about paying it off when they can't afford it just makes no sense. I completely shared the CEO's recommendation of considering more grants to qualified applicants and their families. Then our message becomes something like this: "You justified the need for a grant. Here it is, now go work on fixing the challenge that you've been facing."

Family Endeavors is another entity devoted to the cause of veterans and their families. It is especially helpful in addressing the needs of veterans who are homeless or suffering from PTSD or other challenges. I strongly support their efforts, including their partnership with the Steven and Alexandra Cohen Foundation and its Cohen Veterans Network. That project is dedicated to forming a national network of free mental health clinics for military veterans and their families. One of the first facilities opened in San Antonio.

I've also sought to address the major needs of veterans and their families through the Lackland Fisher House. The Fisher House is a home-away-from-home for the families of seriously injured or ill patients receiving treatment at medical centers on the Lackland base or at other medical facilities in San Antonio. During my stopovers at Lackland, I like to walk into any one of the Fisher Houses on the base unannounced, just to say hello to the dedicated staff there and to thank them for their contributions to those who serve and their loved ones. All services at the Fisher House are completely free. So that's a very direct way to make a difference in the lives of recruits and veterans.

One way or another, I find myself at Lackland on a regular basis. When I pass under the walkway with the sign that says "Welcome to Lackland Air Force Base, Gateway to the Air Force," I feel as if I am entering another one of my homes. So much happened for me at Lackland: going through basic training and Officer Training School, the birth of my son, various assignments when I was headquartered there, or spent considerable time on the base while performing my duties. It's still a hotbed of Air Force activity, with 40,000 personnel involved in some kind of training or function there at any given time. That Friday morning basic training graduation ceremony still happens fifty weeks a year, rain or shine, and I still thrive on being there to see those men and women proudly marching on the Enlisted Airmen Walk and taking the oath to begin their own active service in the Air Force. I probably appreciate those moments even more now, after seeing and experiencing the relevance and the value of what is happening for the 30,000-plus who graduate each year.

My connection to Lackland runs so strong that I am currently involved in a project designed to add something to it. I'm a Board member and senior advisor to the Airman Heritage Foundation. Our mission is to envision, raise funds for, and create a new Airman Heritage Museum that will emerge right near the gateway entrance to Lackland Air Force Base. I can't think of any cause closer to who I am and what I most value.

The mission of the Airman Heritage Museum is to collect, research, preserve, interpret and present the Air Force's enlisted corps history, heritage and traditions to develop airmen today and tomorrow. We aim to instill an understanding of and an appreciation for the airmen's history and culture through engaging exhibits, educational and outreach programs and the stewardship of the national historic collection.

Now, some folks both inside and outside of the Air Force are initially unclear about why we need such a museum because we already have the National Museum of the Air Force located at the Wright-Patterson Air Force Base in Dayton, Ohio. That museum carries its own mission to conserve, interpret and present Air Force history, heritage and traditions. So what's different? The museum in Dayton is not designed primarily to honor enlisted members and their distinguished history. If you talk to almost any accomplished pilots, they will tell you that they can't fly an airplane that isn't well maintained and that pilots don't maintain them—enlisted people do. The Heritage Museum cele-brates the regular airmen, the men and women who perform so many tasks and duties vital to the day-to-day functions, the spirit and the success of the Air Force. Often the ordinary airman is not fully appreciated, and as someone who served more than thirteen years in the enlisted corps, I cherish the idea of validating their contributions in a dynamic way.

We already have a Heritage Museum at Lackland, but it's only about 7,000 square feet and is only able to offer a snapshot look at the history of airmen going back to service performed many years before I came to basic training in 1965. There's an exhibit for the Green Monster, the station where I got my first military cloth-ing issued to keep in my wardrobe and foot locker in the old bar-racks, as well as a number of other replicas. The new museum we seek to build will be 85,000 square feet, providing a full spectrum of our Air Force's enlisted heritage, capturing the airman's journey through the ages. We've got three tractor-trailers of artifacts just waiting for their new home.

The museum will do more than offer history. It will also include an active center for character development and leadership training, so that it's not just something that captures the past. I'm especially excited to imagine how it will be for every recruit in basic training to have the opportunity to walk through this exhibit and see a colorful and complete picture of what they are joining and the tradition they will help to carry on.

We've got the site approved, with permission to move the boundary of the Lackland gate so that folks can visit the museum without going through the security needed to enter the base. All we have to do now is raise $50 million to make this dream a reality. There are naysayers out there who say it will never happen, that those of us promoting this mission will be long gone before it ever comes to fruition. Well, I avoid the word "never" in my vocabulary. Never only applies if you don't do anything. It's like learning to walk—you never move forward unless you take a step. Anyway, I remember the thousands of naysayers when I was young who said the same thing about our nation's mission to go to the moon. We're going to build this museum to honor airmen, and it's going to happen sooner rather than later. I am personally determined to see this happen because this is a very powerful way for me to give back for everything that I gained from being part of this great Air Force. After all, as I say all the time, I am just Airman Ordinary.

There are so many organizations that are working tirelessly to enhance opportunities for military veterans and those facing economic and educational hardship, I sometimes find it hard to say no when I am asked for my time and energy to help. I've tried to limit the number of boards I will commit to at any given time. That also allows me greater opportunities to accept one-time speaking engagements for many different kinds of schools, groups, businesses and organizations. I'll cover that territory more completely in the next chapter.

Juggling these speaking and volunteering commitments with my own personal goals and home life is a new kind of challenge for me, but I am determined to rise up to it. I'll just continue to find my way in balancing my desire to make a difference and my need to slow down enough to smell the roses...before I'm buried under them.

CHAPTER

10

FLOWERISMS: COMMON SENSE TOOLS FOR ACHIEVING UNCOMMON SUCCESS

I'VE ALWAYS BELIEVED in keeping things simple. As an Air Force officer, I tried to make sure that my communication was clear and succinct—no complicated messages, no wasted words. When guiding and mentoring others in my command, I would often refer to basic little sayings I had learned back in rural North Carolina, or others that I had picked up from here, there or everywhere. Some I even came up with myself. Those who served with me would respectfully kid me about these "Flowerisms" and suggest that my ideas were just common sense. My response: "Common sense is uncommon if it's unused."

So when it comes to naming the secrets to success for anyone seeking to overcome hardships and challenges and claim a fulfilling career and a satisfying life, I follow the same simple approach. It's no different when I'm asked to identify the keys to effective leadership. The answers are pretty basic and can be easily spelled out, which I often do, literally, in my speaking engagements. For those reading this book while looking for a way to better themselves, and for those striving for a successful career as a leader inside or outside of the military, I will share some of those simple, basic tools here.

Let's begin by looking at what anyone needs in order to achieve any degree of success in life, no matter how positive or negative your background and environment may happen to be. You may recall me saying that when I first started out in the Air Force, I recognized that the one factor that would determine how far I could go and how much I could achieve was attitude. Do I still believe that's true? Absolutely. So the first advice I would offer to anyone who may be struggling to chart their own life path really comes back to the values and wisdom that my grandmother shared with me back on the farm in Jones County.

"Son, mother wit and honesty will carry you a long way," she would say. "Always do what's right and treat people the way you want to be treated. If you do the wrong thing or you take advantage of someone, that will come back to bite you at some point in your life. So do what's right, be honest, play fair, and remember: integrity, integrity, integrity. And most importantly, maintain a good, positive attitude."

I don't know of anyone that I want to be around who has a bad attitude, but I know a lot of people with good, positive attitudes that I love being around. As I tell students and other young people, a bad attitude will equate to low altitude. You just won't climb very high.

It's important to remember that attitude is a personal choice. No one makes us have a good or bad attitude. We make ourselves have whatever we have and be whatever we're going to be through our attitude. If you elect to approach life with a bad attitude, you need to understand that you are negatively influencing those around you. As a result, folks just don't want to spend time with you. They don't want to invest extra time and energy to guide you or mentor you. In so many ways, you lose out on what you could be gaining in your desire to build a better life for yourself.

It's a simple reality that if you want to change your life, you start by changing your attitude. Our attitude controls our thoughts and our thoughts dictate our actions. Those actions create positive reactions that send ripples out in every direction in our lives.

A few years ago, I was speaking about attitude to a group of students enrolled in KIPP San Antonio, part of a growing network of free, college preparatory public charter schools grooming students from under-served communities for success in college and in life. I spelled out the need to have the right APPROACH:

A – Attitude. You simply must commit to a positive attitude.

P – Perform. Your performance in and out of the classroom needs to always be your very best.

P – Passion. You need to engage fully in your education.

R – Respect. That means respect for teachers and everyone around you.

O – Ownership. You take full responsibility for your education and what you get out of it.

A – Actions. The way that you act reflects your commitment to your education.

C – Commitment. Your commitment to education must be ongoing and unquestioned.

H – Humility. Arrogance will take you where you don't want to go, but humility can carry you further than you might imagine.

I told them about my attitude when I first started earning $94 per month working in an Air Force warehouse. While others spent their money entertaining themselves, I chose to save $30 out of that monthly check because I knew that investing in my future was more important than having a good time in the present.

Again, it all starts with attitude and the choices you make every day. As a finance guy, I've always looked at life as a checkbook. The past is a cashed check, the future is a promissory note and the present is the only thing you can cash. If you do what's right today then whatever happened to you in the past, no matter how difficult it may have been, does not matter as much, and your future will be steered in the right direction.

Another occasion when I was reflecting on the value of a positive attitude occurred when I was speaking at a high school reunion at Jones High School in North Carolina. The theme of the gathering of multiple graduating classes was remembering the past, but in my talk I emphasized the importance of not living in the past. We need to remember the past but live in the present, while preparing for the future. In that audience, many attendees like me had grown up educationally, socially and economically challenged. But when we remembered our past, we could acknowledge that although there was some bad, there was also some good. Most of us had caring parents or grandparents, supportive teachers and a strong sense of community. We learned values that stuck with us. Because of our background, we were resilient and developed a tenacity that we applied to our work and to every life situation. If we had carried a bad attitude when we were growing up and entering adulthood, we would only have seen and paid attention to the bad. That's how you sabotage your own chances for success.

If you faced struggles as a young person, you can choose to obsess about that and feel victimized by what you did not have. You can use it as an excuse for failure in the present and future. But if you choose to be grateful for anything positive that you did have, you will recognize how you have gained tools that will help you get where you want to go.

In my upbringing, I did not have the resources to obtain a college education. I did not have the socialization process that children have in big cities, where a child can learn and grow from more interactions with his peers. Most of my interactions were with the old folks at church or in the fields. I understood that my opportunities were lacking in some ways, but I also appreciated what I did have: a lot of love and people who taught me values, ethics and the need to have respect for people of all ages and backgrounds. Then I set out to take those values and fuse them with intelligence and training to help myself become a better person and to assist others in bettering themselves.

It's easy to go around talking about how life isn't fair. What you want to avoid is letting your view of unfairness, and your emphasis on how bad things were, inhibit your progress and your opportunities for success. The reality is that life won't ever be fair; if you wait for fairness chances are you will be deceased before you find it. Anyway, fair is an abstract concept. It's in the eye of the beholder, the person who is determining what fair is for *them*. So rather than thinking about what's not fair in your life, spend that time and energy trying to learn something, seek to get better in school and in whatever you do, and encourage others around you to do better. You still might be dealing with situations that may seem unfair, but the difference is that your positive attitude will elevate you above that feeling and carry you toward something better. That's what you really want anyway, right?

I know that it can be hard to adopt the right perspective toward the difficulties life brings. You just have to find the courage to take the step that others around you may not have taken by recognizing that there will always be struggles and challenges in life but that you can rise above them. If you have grown up poor, that's something you didn't have a choice in. But if you have the desire to do better and adopt the right attitude toward creating opportunities for yourself, you can begin to chart a different course. If you were marginally educated because you attended schools with inferior resources in areas of a high population of minorities, it may be true that you didn't benefit from the best learning materials or educational environment. But what you do have is a brain, and you can draw upon the desire and motivation to use it to better yourself.

If you have come from a challenging social environment, it is natural that this hardship will have an impact on how you think and the way you see the world. But that does not have to remain the case. You can begin to see that the environment in which you grew up in did impact you, as mine did for me, but that doesn't have to determine how your entire life unfolds. I believe that there is always something positive that emerges out of any bad situation. The way you grew up is something you will always live with but it need not be what you live *by*. Your future is not behind you. That's why they call the past the past.

When I began serving in the Air Force, my goal was to retire as a Chief Master Sergeant. I believed that because of my background, my prospects for advancement would always be limited. I discovered, however, that as you go through life, changes occur. You see the world differently from how it looked while you were growing up. You see yourself differently, too. You can practice what I call "thinking forward" rather than stopping and becoming complacent, or thinking backwards toward what you came out of. You realize that you don't have to stay where you are, with the belief that it is the highest possible plateau for "somebody like me," unless you elect to do so. And if you elect to do so, then you ought to think about why you are making that choice when your own eyes and ears show you that there may be something better for you, something more. If you have the awareness that your past really does not have to limit you, and combine that with the desire to do better and a tangible reason for wanting to achieve more, you can go further than you ever dreamed possible.

Change becomes possible because of your changed mindset. You can't do what you can't think, and you can't achieve what you can't believe. But when you believe that you can do something beyond what your past may tell you that you can do, and you put the effort into making it happen, you will begin to experience new levels of success. Then, when you achieve some successes, it leads you to want to achieve new successes. Before you know it, you've accomplished something that you may have thought you could do but could not see how.

I became a two-star General in the Air Force, but I will be the first to admit that I was no genius. I'm still not the sharpest knife in the drawer, but I know the difference between a knife and a fork. I built on what I did have, without regard for any ways that my past may have impacted me. That's how it can be for you, too.

Sometimes the change that opens the door to success is not just about adjusting your mindset about where you lived and what you lived in. It can also be a matter of actually changing where you live.

It boggles my mind when I see and talk to people back in the rural areas of eastern North Carolina where I grew up, or other impoverished places all over the country, and they tell me that they believe they have achieved all the success that's possible for them when they're working at a fast-food restaurant and living in the same neighborhood or community where they grew up. They may be in their late teens, or twenty-something or even much older, and they have no interest or desire in doing things like attending their local community college and exploring new places to go to and better opportunities to pursue. They just don't believe that something better is out there waiting for them, and they can't see themselves moving away from their poor but familiar environment to go get it.

I don't really understand what's holding them back. I can't help thinking back to when I was a child lying awake in my bed late at night, swatting the mosquitoes that came in from the holes in our tin roof and saying to myself, "I can't believe everyone lives this way, and I'm going to figure out how to live differently someday." What I want to tell anyone stuck in that complacent mindset, believing that they can never get out of their environment and may as well as not try, is this:

The first thing you should do when you realize
you're on a dead horse is get off.

That horse isn't going to move. It's dead. And how do you get off a dead horse? You climb down, fall down, roll down—you just get off somehow. Then you start figuring out what you're going to do and where you're going to go next.

So when you don't see a way out of what you're in, whether it's geographically, economically or socially, get off the dead horse. Commit to getting out. Do something positive. Take a class. Move somewhere where you can find a better job. Seek out and talk to elders or others you may find who did achieve success after coming out of a similar environment. How did they do it? What did they learn? What did they see or understand that you can begin to open up to? What can they offer you that may assist you in changing how you think, what you believe and maybe where you live?

As you meet with these individuals, you can practice another tool to success: striving to be a good listener. One of my Flower-isms comes into play here: "There's a good reason God gave us two ears and one tongue. It means we should listen twice as much as we talk." This can be difficult for young people today, especially in the world of social media where everyone seems to be rushing to spout their opinion, comment on what's hot or vent about some person or situation. They're not contributing to their success. Instead, they need to be listening to adults who are committed to educating and guiding them. That's what you can do when you seek out those who can help you get unstuck. Really listen to what they say and what it may mean to you.

Then, after gathering these insights and inspiration, ask your-self this question: What is one thing I can do today to demonstrate to myself that I am moving forward in my life? Keep asking that question every day. With a positive attitude and a commitment to focus on what you can do, you may be surprised at the kind of success awaiting you.

Almost Anyone Can Become a Leader

With my proven record of achievement as a military officer, I am often asked by groups and organizations to reflect on the keys to effective leadership. The first thing I tell them is that there's noth-ing complicated about leadership. I have found that if you try to complicate it, and describe leadership purely on an intellectual level, you lose people.

I also believe that almost anyone can become a leader if they set that as a goal in their career or life. In my childhood days, if you were down in the dirt playing marbles and you picked up your marble and moved from one circle to another and other people followed you, then you were a leader. Those who aren't leaders, even if they think they are, are those that no one wants to follow. Instead of leading, they're just taking a walk.

Too many people are discouraged from seeking leadership opportunities because they have been told they lack the cognitive skills, the general intelligence or the personality to be a leader. Maybe they grew up in an environment where most people weren't going far in life and there were very few models of those who had been able to step into any positions of leadership. So they may conclude, "I'm a loser, not a leader." Well, both those words start with an "L" but they don't get you to the same place.

There are two ways to change the picture: education and communication. When you actively seek the best educational opportunities available to you and do your best to make the most of them, you begin to acquire the cognitive skills and the understanding that you may have been lacking. If you perform well in the classroom, teachers and mentors will provide you more ways to learn and grow, and others around you may start asking you how you did it. You're already becoming a leader. Education opens up your view of the world and your understanding of how to navigate it. You begin to see possibilities that you couldn't see before.

Education is a key tool for success in leadership and in any aspect of your work and career life, and it's there to assist you at any stage of your progression. When I was in the Air Force enlisted force, obtaining a college degree was the first prerequisite to apply for Officer Training School. Down the road, when I expanded my studies and earned advanced degrees I was better positioned to be considered for assignments with more responsibility and a greater potential to exercise and enhance my leadership abilities. So keep looking for the options within your grasp to further your education.

Learning and practicing excellent communication skills is another tool to hone your leadership ability. You need to get better and better at communicating what you think, what you want, what you believe, what you see and what you can do. All that starts with improving how well you communicate with yourself. If you can't communicate with you, you can't communicate with anybody else. If you have something important in your head, you need to know how to get it out and share it appropriately and effectively. Keep in mind that some people who do a lot of talking aren't really communicating. Choose your words and your points of emphasis with clear, positive goals in mind. When you communicate well with others, they will understand you better, which is critical whether those other people are your superiors, your peers or those you are already leading.

Effective communication also means paying attention to how others are communicating with you. Remember, God gave you those two ears to listen. Seek to understand what people are saying to you, or what they are communicating through their actions. When you're not clear, ask questions. People respond to you more favorably when they detect your sincerity in wanting to know what they're trying to communicate.

When you improve your communication, you become more aware of what is happening all around you. That awareness will enable you to know what to do and how to respond to diverse people and situations. When you get good at that, you are definitely on your way to becoming an excellent leader.

Spelling Out the Keys to Successful Leadership

When you adopt the mindset that you can be a leader and you have the desire to cultivate your leadership ability, you will be better prepared to understand and practice the other keys to successful leadership. Again, the most important part of being a leader really is pretty simple. As I discussed in naming the guiding phi-losophy that I carried with me while rising through the ranks as an Air Force officer, a good leader is someone who is committed to trying to help people reach their full potential. An effective leader maintains that goal as his or her priority, rather than getting wrapped up in what they can do or gain for themselves.

But how do you become really proficient at igniting the best performance of your people? How do you earn their confidence and trust so that they are receptive to what you can offer them? Allow me to share a few more Flowerisms to spell out some of the important ideas. Let's look first at that word LEADER:

L – Loyalty. Make sure that your people know that you are there for them today, you'll be there for them tomorrow, and you'll be there for them when you all get where you need to go in your mission.

E – Enthusiasm. If you don't show passion for what you're doing and how you are relating to your people, they won't follow you. When you are passionate about them and your work together, exude that enthusiasm and it will rub off on them.

A – Accessibility. A leader that keeps their door closed is a closet leader. Show your people that you are approachable and that you want them to come to you for clarity of message, for guidance, for an open ear to hear their concerns or ideas.

D – Determined. You've really got to remain determined that your people will succeed and remember that if they are successful, then so will you. They determine what happens to you.

E – Engaging. You become engaging to your people first by being yourself, acting in a natural way as you relate to them rather than putting on some kind of act or show. Then you want to approach them with tenacity about making a difference in their lives and in the work that you all do.

R – Respect. You need to be respectful of everyone you deal with, at all times. Whether things are going well or not so well, your people need you to treat them with respect as human beings doing their best. If your respect is not genuine, however, they will see it and tune you out. Real respect should be part of your natural manner as a leader.

Another way to grasp what is most essential in building your leadership skills is to envision your role as someone intent on leading with HEART:

H – Humility. Leaders who do not remain humble in exercising their authority demonstrate arrogance, which will kill any enthusiasm or commitment from your people. You can exercise strength as a leader without having to puff yourself up. When you lead from your heart, with a humble approach, people just naturally gravitate toward you. Humility also means you recognize that your intelligence does not make you superior or destined for success. No matter how smart you are or aren't, it is your people that will lift you up and take you further along your leadership trail.

E – Enthusiasm. Another way to look at this trait is that if you don't have the passion for what you're doing and the people you're leading, you ought to be doing something else.

A – Attitude. The importance of a positive attitude never decreases as you climb up any ladder of leadership rungs. Whether you are in a position or assignment that you love or one that was not your preference, you need to approach it with the same attitude. You have a job to do, your people have their part to play, and you're going to devote yourselves to doing the best you can with it every day.

R – Respect. You might see this as a commitment to see the good in everyone so that you can draw out more of what people most have to offer. And remember, even as a leader you can and should be learning from all those around you. That's one more reason for you to respect them.

T – Trust. Your ability to demonstrate that you are leading with heart will help your people trust you. On the other end, you need to trust everyone on your team. If you don't trust someone under your leadership, it's best for everyone if they don't remain there.

I want to highlight that point about seeing the good in everyone and committing to build on what people can do best. It's important that your commitment to bringing out everyone's full potential is inclusive. In other words, taking care of your people means taking care of *all* of them—not just your shining stars. Sure, you want to support those who naturally excel at what they do so you can build on the strengths of your team. At the same time, you also need to help any perceived weaker team members become more productive so that they also have an opportunity to shine. The person who struggles today may be the individual that saves your bacon tomorrow. Invest in those people who don't always seem to get it right. Learn their goals and desires and how you can best support them in reaching them. Offer them time and encouragement, show them that you believe in them, and utilize your mentoring skills to boost their morale and their performance. Remember, that fast trotter at the front of your pack may trip someday and the donkey who started at the back may wind up leading the pack.

As I've said before, none of us are smart enough to lead successfully by ourselves. The people we take care of will take care of us, and when our people have a positive perception of who we are and how we carry ourselves it translates into a greater performance on our part as leaders. We earn a positive reputation for the way we reach those with whom we serve with our unswerving commitment to do so.

Now we'll zoom in on that word COMMITMENT:

C – Communicate. Regardless of whom you are dealing with, or what situation you need to navigate, effective communication will always be critical to interpersonal relations. Falling into old habits in how you communicate with those around you can undermine your relationships and your ability to guide and mentor them. And never make the mistake of believing that you communicate by means of your status. You don't. You have to communicate as a person reaching other people.

O – Obligate. When you're committed to something, you've got to obligate yourself to stay with it. In accounting terms, a commitment is an administrative reservation of funds while an obligation is a legal liability to pay somebody. In leadership, a commitment without a real obligation behind it is just an activity. It needs that sense of obligation to make it productive.

M – Motivate. First, you've got to be motivated yourself about what you're doing. Then you need to motivate those around you to want to reach their full potential. When you try to make a difference in their lives and guide and support them to perform to the best of their ability, your sincerity must always shine through.

M – Mentor. When I talk about being a good mentor, I always emphasize the difference between a mentor and a sponsor. A sponsor is somebody who carries others on their back and opens doors for them. A mentor is somebody that people can call late at night and say, "I'm not sure about something. What do you think? How would you handle this situation?" Mentors are always there, in good times and bad, exhibiting caring and respect for you as a person as well as a team member.

I – Integrity. As a leader, you may come face to face with new temptations where doing something you know is not right appears to be just what you need to get ahead. Ignore those temptations.

Like my grandmother told me, straying from your integrity will always come back to bite you.

T – Trust. Your people have to believe they can trust you and you have to know you can trust them. Trust must remain a level and even exchange if you're going to succeed together. You also need to trust their ability to tap their potential. You do this by seeing that potential even when they can't see it themselves.

M – Modesty. Some leaders try to intimidate people or embarrass them, making them feel less than they are. They forget that you catch more flies with honey than you do with vinegar. Keep in mind that you never have it all figured out. No matter what title you carry or what level you have achieved, you still need people. That person you walk past without noticing might be the one that lifts you up. If you're sincere and humble toward everyone, and you simply tell the truth when dealing with them, you stand a much better chance of being a positive enabler in the lives of those you lead and them being a positive enabler in your career and life.

E – Engaging. Make it clear that you honestly seek to engage with your people, not just tell them what to do or what not to do. Show them you care about them as people and consider it your job to support, encourage and guide them to the best of your ability.

N – Natural. Again, you are who you are. You can act like someone else, you can try to look like someone else, but you can't be anyone else. If you're not natural, you just look funny, act funny and sound funny. Leading is not about being funny. It's about being real, and trying to help whoever you can along the way. When you act natural, it also gives your people more permission to be who they are, rather than trying to be someone else in the name of impressing you, which makes them more likely to perform at their best.

T – Tenacity. When you believe you can make a positive difference in someone's life, do not give up. Sometimes that team member who is struggling had a previous leader who took one shot at helping them and then moved on. When you make it clear that you're determined and committed to hang in there with them, they will rise up to fully receive what you have to offer.

Related to that last point, sometimes colleagues would question my tenacious commitment to keep working with those who weren't performing or who made mistakes. "They're just misfits; you need to get rid of them," they would argue. I would respond with a finance reference. "We should not write somebody off just because they didn't make the first payment. I don't want to write them off unless it's in a serious delinquent status." There's good in everybody. Go that extra mile to try to find it and bring more of it out. Only let them go when you know you have gone the extra mile or more in assisting them, and then accept that this individual is simply a good bad example of those rare occasions when someone does not work out.

I am often asked by those who are already in positions of leadership in the military how they can become a two-star General. I share with them many of the same ideas we have been exploring here. Then I emphasize to them that rising to higher levels of leadership also has to do with the ability and desire to learn from your experiences so you can keep building on your SUCCESSES:

S – Sensitive. This is not an obvious trait for many leaders. I have found that to be a really successful leader you must be sensitive to the reality that everybody doesn't look like you, think like you, act like you or come from the same background and same kinds of life experiences as you. If you want to successfully lead them, you need to realize and respect that reality and find a way to effectively relate to those who are especially different from you.

U – Understanding. Once you cultivate that sensitivity, you are much better prepared to add the important layer of understanding.

If you are able to figure out that someone's struggles to perform or to be initially receptive to you can be traced to their personal background or beliefs, you've got a head start on making the right connection with them so you can assist them in their role in fulfilling your team's mission.

C – **Compassion.** It comes back to humility and recognizing that you don't have all the answers for someone you may be relating to. If you approach them with compassion, you make it easier for them to find their own answers for any issues or roadblocks that may be keeping them from doing their best.

C – **Concern.** If you are struggling to understand someone, and they are struggling to understand you, try to demonstrate a genuine concern for the problem and a commitment to see it through. Show them that you regard both of you as equals and that it's important to you as their leader that you each keep talking and listening to get where you need to be.

E – **Ethical.** To me, good leaders should always do the right thing in every situation. It should be clear and obvious. Yet I do not believe everyone feels this way, and some say it depends on the situation. That still doesn't change my belief and I hope it doesn't change yours.

S – **Silence.** To really listen and hear what our people are trying to communicate to us, we need to be silent. Some leaders believe they must do most of the talking and just can't shut up. They forget that you can't hear with your lips. When you're silent, you listen with both your head and your heart.

S – **Sincerity.** If your people believe you are not sincere, they may play games with you. I don't know about you, but I'm not about playing games. Always be sincere in how you act, how you engage people, how you mentor them and how you seek to motivate them to reach their full potential.

E – Excellence. If you're really striving for excellence in your performance as a leader, satisfactory is just a stop along the way. You're not where you want and need to be until you truly have achieved excellence, which is reflected by how well your people are doing.

S – Standards. We should always have very specific standards for what we want to achieve ourselves and what we are looking for from others as a measure of their success. Make sure your people know and understand your standards and communicate them clearly and consistently.

Contrasting Military and Civilian Leadership

All of these tools and traits for effective leadership can be applied whether you happen to be building a leadership career in the military or in the civilian ranks. Since I have recently worked in the corporate world, I have had a chance to explore and discover what's similar and what's different about performing as a leader in the two environments.

First, the missions are very different. In the corporate world, your primary missions are to satisfy the customers and try to make a profit. In the military, your mission is service, or to put it another way, your mission is whatever the mission is. There is no profit, only the achievement of fulfilling the mission assigned to you.

On the corporate side, you are expected to satisfy your customers who invest in your product or service. In the military, your customers are really the American people and you satisfy them by doing your part in serving our great nation.

Leaders in the civilian ranks are motivated to help their business or organization make money. Military leaders are motivated to be servants.

Civilian leaders tend to have a great deal of control over their own career trajectory. Once they establish a track record of success, they decide how long to stay with any employer and when and where to go when they see an opportunity for advancement or fulfillment. On the other side, military leaders serve in whatever capacity and in whatever assignment they are given by those above them. There is very little if any choice.

As a leader in the military, you follow orders delivered by your commander. As long as those orders are legal, moral and ethical, you are trained to do what you are told and have taken an oath to do so. You don't get to choose your bosses. As a civilian leader, if you don't like what your boss is telling you to do, or you believe he or she lacks the kind of values that matter most to you, you simply spruce up your resume and start making contacts to find a new boss in some other work environment. And before it comes to that, you often have an opportunity to try to go against the grain— to communicate your displeasure and seek a change in approach or direction by your boss, your business or both. That's not the way it works when you're wearing a military uniform.

Because military leaders follow orders and give orders, they tend to take a strategic view to fulfill the mission. Civilian leaders are more apt to approach decisions with an operational or tactical view. Their thinking and decision-making may be more flexible or fluid.

So the differences are clearly defined and significant. And yet, as someone who has now worked in both realms, I can also point to many similarities of being a leader in military and civilian environments.

First, it's important to note that while your immediate superiors in the military also serve in the military, the Commander in Chief of all the armed forces is a civilian: the President of the

United States. Regardless of that person's beliefs, party, affiliation or the presence or absence of any prior military experience, that individual is still the leader of the military. As a military leader, your function at any given time and your entire career may well be impacted by the priorities and decisions of one or more Commanders in Chief that you serve under through the years.

In terms of your day to day approach to leading, the main similarity is that in both environments you are still working with people. In the corporate world, just as it is in the military, it is still your job to do your best to train, educate, guide, encourage and mentor the people on your team so that they perform at their best and advance toward the fulfillment of their own goals and objectives. You are there to be of service to those who serve or work with you.

When I accepted my first civilian position after retiring from the Air Force, I took the same personal approach to mentoring that guided me as a military officer. For some newcomers to our business, it was a bit of a surprise when I would go out onto the floor, pull up a chair next to someone on my team and simply ask them how they were doing and what was going on yesterday, today and tomorrow. I wasn't there to call them on the carpet for something that had gone wrong, which may be the only reason for some leaders to spend individual time with one of their people. I was building interpersonal relationships. And whether it's a business environment or a military base, people will tell you what you need to know to be the most effective leader you can be in that domain when you show that kind of personal interest in them.

So what I discovered in working for a business is that I was still the same person with the same values and qualities that I had been when I was working at the Pentagon or commanding the Second Air Force. I still had the same reason for being there, and the same objective of trying to make a difference in people's lives. I led with the same style—seeking to encourage others, finding ways to break things down to what really matters, communicating with them clearly and consistently. I took the same personal, caring approach. I gained further evidence that when you are operating as a senior leader, whether in the military or as a civilian, what sets you apart from others, what really makes you effective, is how people perceive you, how they respect you and endear themselves to you, and how you make them feel.

I even followed the same approach in dealing with email and social media. My theory about email communication is that the E does not really stand for electronic. It refers to *evidence*. Any email that you send can be used to do you harm just as easily as it can be helpful in communicating a message. It's instantly and permanently public, so you don't want to put anything in there that you wouldn't want to read on the front page of the *Washington Post*. And it can be altered after you let it go. That's why anyone who has worked with me knows that when I reply to one of their emails, the answer will be very brief: yes, no, maybe or come see me and we'll talk about it. Not only is email potentially dangerous, it's also less personal. It's the same with texting. As the Air Force Budget Director, I reached the point of having to ask all my attendees at my staff meetings to leave their electronic devices outside the door when they came in. I had to take that step because in previous meetings I had witnessed staff members texting one another across the table. So while technology can and should be used appropriately to enhance efficiency, leaders need to remember the vital importance of personal communication.

In the big picture, it doesn't really matter whether you are operating from within the military or inside some corporate or civilian entity. You can be the same kind of leader, just in a different environment. You can lead with heart. You can use common sense. You can always practice integrity. You can listen with both ears. You can exude your enthusiasm for the work or the mission while also practicing humility, being careful not to get caught up in your own intelligence. You can demonstrate your genuine caring and respect for everyone around you. You can guide people in such a way that they all know they are appreciated, and valued, and that they have a vital part of the "we" within your environment. You can pay attention to the small stuff because we see the elephants but it's the gnats that get in your eyes and make them water.

And yes, you can absolutely dedicate yourself to the mission of helping all your people reach their full potential.

11

How to Successfully Navigate a Military Career

In the Introduction to this book, I named several possible motivations for reading about my story of entering the U.S. Air Force as a seventeen year old and retiring as a Major General and the longest-serving airman in Air Force history. One reason I imagined was to seek guidance and shared wisdom about launching and successfully navigating a military career. If that's what got you here, it's time to listen up. This chapter is for you.

I'm going to walk you from ground zero of this experience all the way through the potential steps of rising through the ranks as a high-level military officer. If you've been reading right along from the start of this book you should already have a pretty clear picture of what military life is all about and how it can serve as a vehicle for major achievement and fulfillment in your life. But now I'm going to stop and spend some extra time zeroing in on many of the most important considerations and action steps that you will need to take on this journey of being of service. Whether a military career is still just an idea floating in your mind, or whether you have already joined the cause of serving our nation, I trust that you will find something useful to assist you.

Let's start at the beginning: the choice to enter the military. For me, it was pretty simple. I wanted to find a way to better myself after growing up with severe economic, social and educational hardships, and two of my cousins had told me about how the military lifted them up. It sounded good to me, so off I went at the age of seventeen. I never looked back until retiring from the Air Force forty-six years later.

Is that how it could go for you? I couldn't tell you that, but if you have not made the leap to join the military yet I can offer some things to think about. First, you would be wise to give some careful consideration as to whether the military is really right for you. I've spent lots of time around basic training at Lackland Air Force Base, and I know that a large number of recruits come in with some background and knowledge of the military. Maybe they had parents, siblings, cousins, aunts or uncles, or good friends who had served. Perhaps they grew up near a military installation and met and talked to those stationed there when they came off base. That kind of exposure certainly can be helpful in gaining some idea of what the military may be like, if you take the time to listen to what others say about their military experience and ask good questions.

Many other times, however, I have met young men and women who believe they are ready to make the commitment to join the military without gaining much background about what they're in for. They have not done their due diligence at all. They have what they believe are very clear ideas about what it will be like to wear the uniform because they've spent hours and hours playing some of those many combat and special ops video games. Their ideas are almost always all wrong. If you think you know all about special ops from what you see and do on a screen, I've got news for you. You know all about the special ops video game; you don't know about special ops. You should not know about special ops because you're not supposed to know unless and until you are ever selected to be part of that critical operation.

So here's the key lesson. The military is not a game. It's serious business. It's nothing to play with, and if you are not comfortable with the possibility that you could be sent off to war someday and even die for your country, find something else to do. There's a price we all must be prepared to pay for our freedom in this great nation.

Many young people today have learned some of the realities about the military from participating in programs such as Junior ROTC or Civil Air Patrol. If you have not made that kind of choice, it doesn't mean you can't be a good fit for the military. It just means you should take the time now to gain a greater awareness about what the military is and what it isn't. Slow down and honestly assess your own strengths and abilities, and think about how military service could align with them. Do you have excellent technical or mechanical skills? Are you a really good communicator? If you have demonstrated skills like that, the military will train you, educate you, and help you obtain the needed certifications in your skill to succeed in the military and someday in the civilian work world, if that is what you decide to do. If there is a field in which you are not yet proficient but have a sincere interest in learning and honing, and you are not inclined to go to college or take some outside training, the military may be the place for you to do so.

Part of your due diligence should be to talk to people who know about the specific service you are thinking about. If you reach out to them, I can reasonably assure you that they will be very willing to share what they know and what they've experienced. They can provide information that you need or clear up things that you may be confused about.

The goal is to gather enough material for you to make an informed decision. You do no one any favors if you join the military when it really is not right for you. Those who screen military candidates do their best to weed out those who don't belong, but they don't always get it right. Don't waste their time or your time by misleading them with incomplete or erroneous information about your background, your beliefs, your life attitude and your goals.

You also need to fully understand and accept that you are making a firm commitment. You can't join the military with the idea that you'll give it a shot and if you don't like it after a little while, or it's not what you thought it would be, you'll get out and move on. The military needs people who are committed to the cause. You've got to be committed to fulfill your agreed upon term of service. You've got to be committed to always doing the right thing. You've got to be committed to taking orders. You've got to be committed to not having things your way in regards to where you're going to go and what you're going to do at any given time. If you're about control, you're entering the wrong business. Unlike the civilian world where you can exercise a fair degree of freedom and flexibility in plotting your course and career, the military expects that you will relinquish that control because you have accepted the concept of service.

Let's break down that word SERVICE:

S - Sacrifice. You commit to performing for the good of the military and others that you serve with, rather than for the good of yourself. If you think this will be about "self" you are "selfish."

E - Efficiency. It is your job to perform to your utmost ability and never waste time or energy, either yours or someone else's. The military must receive the maximum capability from every public dollar entrusted to it, and no matter your rank or job, you have a role to play in that equation.

R - Respect. Always show respect for self and others. Remember that everyone deserves respect no matter their rank, position or assignment, or whether they happen to look, think and act like you or are totally different from you. You may find that a lack of respect may cause some bad luck.

V - Valor. Service requires courage and bravery. You must stand up for right and be ready to serve when and where called upon.

I - Integrity. Regardless of what your habits may have been before joining the military, you must always do the right thing privately and publicly while serving in your chosen branch of the military. There is never any excuse for lack of integrity.

C - Communication. You must listen carefully to everyone, whether they are your peers, your superiors or civilians you interact with. You also need to communicate in a clear, open, honest and thorough manner. Remember, in order to effectively communicate with somebody else you first have to be able to communicate with yourself.

E - Excellence. You must strive to do your utmost best at everything you are asked to do. Your superiors will be quick to remind you that in the military, satisfactory is not a substitute for excellence.

To have a successful military career, you need to do more than simply accept the idea that service is your mission and that you will strive to become a true servant. It's not just about a willingness to serve where needed and when called upon, doing whatever you are asked to do. You also must somehow tap a real passion for service. If you don't have a passion for service, then you may find yourself regarding some assignment or task as just a job. And if it's a job that you don't particularly want to do, you're in trouble.

There were not many days in my career that spanned almost five decades that I actually worked. I served. It was an honorable service that I rendered day in and day out. I had that passion. If you don't come with it or access it early in your military experience, chances are you will leave frustrated. The good news is that you are likely to discover that the longer you serve, the more passionate you'll become about serving. As I became more aware of world affairs and international relationships, I gained a deeper appreciation for the honor of living in a free nation and doing everything that was required to maintain that freedom.

If you enter the military with the simple goal of wanting to improve your life, you may not initially grasp the importance of the contribution you are making in serving our country. Maybe you were poor and simply desired a better standard of living, but you commit to the expectations of being of service and you do your best every day. Soon you are likely to better understand what this idea of service is really all about, how it relates to democracy and aiding our allies around the world. Then you see yourself as being one of millions of servants helping to preserve what really matters. Your passion is fueled.

After you give careful consideration to entering the military and you make the commitment, you must be mentally prepared to face the challenges of basic training. I will use the reference point of the Air Force because that is what I know best, but I can assure you that you will encounter similar challenges and potential obstacles in any service of the Defense Department you may happen to choose.

One of the first challenges will be accepting the discipline that is an essential component of basic training. Your instructors and commanders have a job to do. They need to modify your behavior, to teach you to think and act like a servant as opposed to someone who has just left home or has gotten used to living and working in some civilian work environment. You must understand and accept that you are there to be trained and that you are going to need to take orders, often in a way that may ruffle your feathers. Remember when my trainer said "I am going to be your everything?" If I had rebelled against this manner of asserting authority, or the tone of voice in which the message was conveyed, I would have gotten off on the wrong foot. I might have struggled through basic training and maybe even have become one of the casualties who didn't make it.

There are two things you can do to help yourself get through this initial testing period. The first is to realize that any discomfort you are feeling about the rules and regulations, or the manner in which you are being directed, is going to be temporary. If you stick with it, maintaining a positive attitude, you will find that you'll be treated differently as you continue along with your commitment to serve. As you prove yourself and mature in training, you will notice that the nature of interactions with your superiors and your relationships with them will change.

There's a threshold that you will likely cross, usually just past the halfway point of basic training. During my training, our training commander began to communicate very differently with us at about the five-week mark. He started saying things like, "Okay, you guys are going to be graduating soon. You're going to be full-fledged members of the Air Force. You will be expected to make a great contribution to the nation. We need you. So what we're going to be doing with you soon is to teach you what your particular contribution will be." Some of us might have been left scratching our heads wondering what all that stuff about being our mothers, our fathers, our sisters and our brothers was all about. What it was all about was getting us to the point of being fully ready and capable of doing our part in the Air Force. That could not have happened if that Sergeant had begun with a message like, "Flowers, I'm glad you're here. For the next several weeks I'm going to be treating you real nice, and if I say something you don't like, or in a way that displeases you in any way, just tell me and I will change right away." Nope, that wouldn't have modified our behavior.

So the tough tone and authoritarian presence had a purpose, but it was temporary. You got broken down in order to be built back up. Over time that mission evolved into something else. When you are tempted to leave and run off to somewhere where you will be "treated better than this," keep that reality in mind. Some instructors assist in that process by telling recruits up front that the authoritarian approach of the initial weeks will be a necessary but temporary part of their experience.

The other point to remember is that many people you will be around will not look like you, act like you, think like you, or view life like you. The military experience, beginning with basic training, brings together people from many different backgrounds. It melds people of different races and ethnicities, different religious and political beliefs, and different accents and prejudices. That's true for your peers that you must learn to get along well enough with so that you trust one another and work together as a unit. It's also true for your instructors and commanders. You've got to respect that they are different people, too. Your trainer is not just some mean old person obsessed with trying to convert you to look and act like them and others in authority. They are just people who have been on a different path than you. If you're eighteen or nineteen years old and they are thirty-five of forty, they grew up in a different era. They may be someone more comfortable talking to people directly on the phone rather than texting them on a device. Instead of coming from a background of tweeting or twittering, or playing YouTube videos, they may actually be used to taking the time to write well thought-out notes and communications to be shared in a group of men and women that must be reached and guided effectively. They also may have grown up in a very different social and geographic area than you, and that has shaped them just as yours has shaped you.

We're all different people, but in the military we must learn to come together as one. Every assignment and every mission that you will be part of relies on that unity. If you learn to accept and even embrace the idea that you will always find yourself in close quarters with people very different from you, and that your success will be in their hands, you will discover that diversity is a strength.

Once you pass the test of basic training, the next challenge will be to learn to accept early assignments that may not be your first preference. That may begin with your assignment for technical training, which might not be your first choice. Then you're going to be sent somewhere for your first job. When you get there you may look around and decide that you don't like it because it's too cold there, or there are not enough African Americans there, or there are not enough white people there, or there are not enough women. Once again, you can help yourself with the reminder that this too is temporary. You're not going to be at this place on this assignment for your entire military career. The military journey is one of rapidly shifting terrain and environments, and those who succeed are those who learn to roll with the changes.

Keeping a positive attitude also will enable you to realize that the folks that have sent you on a particular assignment know more than you do about how you fit into the greater needs of the military. So you need to approach your assignments with the understanding that you are doing it for the greater good. Everyone has a role to fulfill in the military, just like on a football or basketball team. Taking on your role with your full heart is part of being that servant you committed to being. The funny thing is, once you make up your mind to truly accept what you are given even when it's not where you want to be or doing what you want to be doing, most of the time it works out really well. You may be surprised that when it comes time to leave that place you never wanted to be in the first place, you're actually sad to go. You know that you have been making a contribution and you don't want it to end.

When you understand that acceptance is an essential reality of service, you also will be better positioned to be entrusted with greater responsibilities and more important assignments. If you learn your job, hone your skill, exhibit respect and a positive attitude toward everyone around you, you may be awarded opportunities for advancement. In the Air Force, once you reach the rank of E-4 (Senior Airman) you may be considered for Airman Leadership School.

At this point you may be crossing another threshold. It may be your first opportunity to look at yourself as a potential leader and discover what you may have in your own leadership tool kit. It's also where your passion for service may get another boost, because you see that you can make a greater contribution than you may have imagined. Others will be assessing your potential as well, and if they like what they see you will get a chance to show more.

When you are promoted to the E-5 level (Staff Sergeant), you will be able to develop your supervisory skills, and if you perform well over time you may be chosen to become a Technical Sergeant (E-6). That was a challenging progression for me. I reached Staff Sergeant in four years, but it took me six years to rise to Tech Sergeant. That could have been a real roadblock in my leadership career if I had allowed it to be, but I held onto that attitude that had sustained me: every obstacle is just a speed bump to success. That's the kind of attitude that will carry you to greater heights in your military career too.

Everyone has different goals in life, and in the military, so how high you climb in the ranks may be guided by personal choice as well as how others perceive you and your potential. In the Air Force, many airmen retire at the E-5, E-6 or E-7 (Master Sergeant) level. They still had a distinguished period of service and most likely made vital contributions. That may be your experience on your own military path. Then again, you may demonstrate leadership ability that enables you to reach higher. There are goals set for you by virtue of rank all along the way, and if you meet those goals and maintain a reputation as someone who will do things the right way, you may be promoted to serve as an E-8 (Senior Master Sergeant) and even an E-9 (Chief Master Sergeant) someday. Then you become the leader of the leaders of the airmen in the enlisted corps.

There may be even more in store for you. If you entered the military with only a high school education but you now have taken advantage of opportunities to obtain a college degree, you will be eligible to apply for Officer Training School and embark on a further leg of the journey as a military officer. It doesn't matter when you take that leap. Remember, it took me more than thirteen years to make OTS, although my situation was certainly not typical.

So far we have been tracing the route you may follow if you entered the military without a college degree, which is the situation for a large percentage of military recruits. Perhaps they could not afford college or just didn't see college as the right way for them to go, or they did enroll in a college or university but found that they were not going to be able to do everything it took to graduate. That's when the military emerged as a viable option. However, some men and women begin their military journey after obtaining a college degree, meaning they may become a commissioned officer. If that is your situation, you need to recognize that you will be facing many of the same challenges and potential roadblocks as any airman who advanced through the ranks and earned an opportunity to be trained as a military officer.

You have already heard me describe my various ranks and assignments as a military officer, so you are familiar with some of what it takes to advance to the higher rungs. In the last chapter, we spelled out some of the key traits in becoming a successful leader in any arena, including the military. To highlight a few key points, you've got to consistently perform well, demonstrate unwavering integrity, maintain a humble spirit, and commit to becoming an excellent guide and mentor to those serving with you. Pragmatically, you need to understand the need to go outside of your primary field and diversify in your areas of leadership. You are also expected to further your education by pursuing advanced degrees and training.

As you advance as a military officer, there's something else you need to be prepared for—the constant moving and relocating that comes with being granted new assignments. It often feels as though those new assignments pop up just when you and your family are feeling settled where you are. You can forget about continuity of education for your children or building equity in a home or anything else that comes from investing in one place for an extended period of time.

You also need to accept that the process of obtaining promotions and more important assignments in the military is much different from the civilian world. You don't lobby for bigger titles or more lucrative compensation packages, you wait for higher rank-ing officers to decide where they need to send you and what they need you to do. You are a servant, not a free agent building a career in your own way. In industry you may go from job to job in search of more money, more satisfaction or more whatever, but in the military you are assigned different jobs to learn more, to vary your experience, to follow a career pattern others may have in mind for you. Individual officers or officer boards will decide on the next steps of your path. They will be scrutinizing your perfor-mance in a process that you're not invited to sit in on. You just wait for them to make their decisions. Ironically, that becomes more true the higher you climb.

Certainly you have clues along the way. When you are selected to serve as an executive officer or military aide, you know that you are being looked at for potentially higher positions. Do your job well, commit to the extra hours required and show that you're someone who can be trusted, and you will stand a good chance of continuing to achieve more as you gain higher and higher ranks.

How long will your military career last? That's an individual decision, of course, but often in my role of mentoring others I would recommend that they strongly consider going further down the military road than they were thinking about. Sometimes they would consider leaving because of some frustration with a situa-tion that I knew would be temporary, or that they could rise above. Other times I just saw potential in them that they may not have even seen in themselves. Many of these men and women later expressed their gratitude to me for urging them to stick with it, because they were able to achieve more and serve in a greater capacity than expected.

The way I look at it is that if you're doing something you're passionate about, why wouldn't you want to do it for a long time?

Why would you want to just do it today and stop? If you just do it temporarily, it's like getting intoxicated. You drink tonight to feel good for a short period of time and tomorrow you'll feel bad, even sick. If you want to feel good tomorrow and for a long time, you choose to drink casually or not at all. Don't go for that brief rush that short-term military service can give you. Bring it more fully into your life to experience its sustained rewards.

To me, there's just something about longevity and commitment that short-term ventures will never yield. If you don't give a life experience the time to really mature, you won't ever realize if it was really good, bad, indifferent or something that just happened. That's especially true with a military commitment. I believe that service is an endearment, not something that's going to end tomorrow or next week or next year. Remember, we've been serving in this country since the nation was founded.

You can also look at it through the lens of gaining a return on investment. When you commit to a career in the military, there's a return on investment for you as an individual and a return on investment for the greater good. Personally, you know that you have made a difference for a longer period of time. The return for the greater good for the military is that they invested in you and had a longer period of time to receive the return on that investment. So rather than regarding your military service as something that's here today and gone tomorrow, you might see it as something that's here today and here forever...in some capacity. No matter what else you may do in life, your military background and experience will serve as a valuable rudder in whatever direction you may happen to go in next.

For some people who serve in the military, their length of service is shaped by their ability to adapt to change. Some shake their heads and say they have had enough of all these new technological advances, or the latest rules and regulations, or new roles or expectations triggered by shifting budget priorities, or just some new dynamic they would describe as foolish or unbearable. "I've had a good career but I'm not about to change at this point," they often tell me. I usually reply, "So why do you want to keep living? Change is inevitable until you die."

I experienced many changes in my military career, not only with circumstances around me but with my own ways of looking at things. When I look back to how I saw things twenty or thirty years ago as opposed to how I see them today, I am struck by how much is different. Hopefully I have grown and matured in my perspective, and that maturity is still happening now, several years after I finally decided that after forty-six years, five months and twenty-four days of active service, my military career had run its course.

So if you're just beginning your military service, or thinking about taking this step on your life path, I'm excited for you and the possibilities, and the meaningful rewards that await you. Who knows, maybe after your military experience runs its course someday, you will be motivated to mentor and guide other people who may be about to make that commitment to join the military and be of service.

12

REBUILDING THE VILLAGE

MY WIFE AND I had many choices for where to establish a second home. At different points in my Air Force career we bought property in various attractive locales along the corridor from the greater Washington, DC area down the East Coast, with the idea of someday turning one of them into a second retirement home to complement our primary house in San Antonio. But when it came time to actually commit to one location for this purpose, I decided that the only fitting place to create a second home was....back home.

It all worked out perfectly. Our family held onto the house in North Carolina that my mother was living in when she passed away in 2006. It was only minutes away from the spot where the small, two-bedroom house where my grandparents raised me in Jones County once stood. Within a few years I found myself buying my mother's house, renovating it and shaping it into a very homey second home. It has become a haven for Ida and I to settle into for our North Carolina visits that usually last a week or longer, four times a year. It's a simple house, right across the street from one of the area's schools, but it's well situated for our quick jaunts to the ocean, up to Washington, or to the homes of friends who live a bit further south. We also take short day trips to visit a couple of my sisters from my father's second marriage. More important to me, this second home keeps me firmly connected to my roots.

Being back in the Jones County and Kinston area of eastern North Carolina always reminds me of those long hours under the hot sun picking corn and tobacco on the farm. It takes me back to memories of my school, our church, the woods where we chopped wood and hunted rabbits, my bus driving route on the local roads, and everything and everyone else that were part of my childhood and adolescence in a family of sharecroppers. But I don't come back just to reminisce. By spending so much time in the land of my youth, I also hope that in some way I am making a statement: never forget where you come from. Your roots are not just something to reflect upon now and then. Your roots are who you are.

I don't have nearly as much family back home to visit these days. My brother Uronus still lives in the area and there are a few others I can stop in and say hey to. But most of those whom I was closest to are gone. My Uncle Walter, who was like an older brother to me when we shared a bedroom for many years, passed away in 2016. My grandmother, who persevered through severe health problems for many years after I left home, finally succumbed in 1999. Although she was never physically able to travel to any of the ceremonies where new insignia were pinned on my uniform to mark a new rank, she proudly followed my career through newspaper articles. Every time I visited her, she made sure to show me the latest clippings. I smile now when I recall how for many years Mama would tell everyone she knew that I was doing well in "the Army" because to folks who lived in the country in her time, anyone who served in the military just naturally had to be in the Army. It was only in her later years that we finally got her to say "Kendell's in the Air Force."

When I really want to connect with the extended family that I knew when I was young, I know where I can find them: a place called Hayti. That's a cemetery not far off Route 58 down a side street of disheveled homes. I remember coming there often from the time I was a boy, with clergy and the others from Haughton Chapel Free Will Baptist Church presiding over the burials of one more family member. I must have at least fifty relatives buried there, going back to my great-grandparents. The headstones proclaim the names of Flowers, Roberts, McBynum, Hicks, Brown, Cheston and others. I always linger awhile when I come to the markers for Shade and Lucy Roberts, and this old Air Force General has to admit that the emotions bubble up each and every time. These two humble and hard-working individuals were my parents.

So, yes, I do come back to remember, but I also come back because I believe I can make a difference. That's my primary mission in retirement, and although there is great need and countless opportunities for me to make a difference back in San Antonio and in the many programs that serve the needs of military veterans and their families, it's also important to me to make a difference in the place that was part of me long before I ever wore a uniform.

When I come back home, people are always asking me to speak somewhere. I do my best to say yes as often as I can. It was easy to say yes awhile ago when Mr. Mills, my former science teacher and supporter, asked me to speak at an all-class reunion at my alma mater, Jones High School. It was wonderful to meet up with fellow classmates and others I had known when I was there. Many of them told me how proud they were of me for going further than anyone ever imagined I could go because I was that kid who came off the farm with no resources and, as they believed at the time, no hope for a better life.

One of my former classmates had a son who joined the Air Force, and I've been grateful for the opportunity to mentor him. When he was struggling with his assignment at Grand Forks, which happened to be my first stop after basic training, and he told me how bad it was there, I just said, "But it could be worse. And you don't ever want to look at how bad today is. You want to think about what you can do to make tomorrow better, for yourself and for the nation."

I always make it a point to schedule one of our regular North Carolina visits to coincide with Veteran's Day so I can speak to groups of veterans, their families and others from our community who come out to honor those who served. One year I was even selected to be Grand Marshall for the Veteran's Day parade through Kinston. It was my introduction to the Walk of Honor, where brick pavers note the names of those from Lenoir County and surrounding areas who served our nation. Flags from all five services—Army, Navy, Air Force, Marines, Coast Guard—fly above the exhibit on the banks of the Neuse River, just off Heritage Street. Whenever I'm there I can't help remembering how Heritage Street, with its many shops for the wealthy, was practically off-limits for African Americans when I would go to Kinston on Saturdays. Today it's not far from Chef & The Farmer, the restaurant that gained national notoriety when it was featured on a PBS television program and now attracts people from as far as Texas.

In reality, most of downtown Kinston does not look like a

magnet for celebrity-seekers. Dozens of stores and restaurants have
been abandoned or boarded up. Many of the homes just off the
main thoroughfares are in such disrepair they should be torn
down, but people still live in most of them. The Trailways sign still
stands at the location of the bus station at Blount and Indepen-
dence where I rode off to Raleigh as a seventeen year old on the
way to begin my life in the Air Force, but the bus station isn't
there. So much of Kinston is run down, ignored, suffering. It was
no surprise awhile back when I heard that Kinston had the highest
per capita crime rate in the state of North Carolina.

The scene isn't any more encouraging when I drive by the
places I used to know in Jones County. Many families live in ram-
shackle houses. Some things have changed since my childhood,
others haven't. Kids don't have much to do, and many of them do
things they shouldn't. I guess that's one area where circumstances
were a little better for us growing up. We didn't have much to do
either, at least compared to kids in other places, but you don't
know what you don't know. Most of what we knew about life
came from what we saw in the country or in the tiny town of Trenton, or from those occasional Saturday pilgrimages to the "big
city" of Kinston. Crime was not so much of an issue in my genera-
tion because we were kept so busy working on the farms and
because respect and discipline were ingrained in us. We were kept
safe and supported by the village.

Today, the village as a social and environmental force is missing. I see and feel that void every time I come back. As it is in most
of our country, extended families no longer hold tight as glue. Kids
from homes where their parents didn't stay together don't have
loving and caring adults to step in and fill the void. Many who are
struggling just slip through the cracks.

Even the church is no longer a stabilizing and unifying force in the community. When we attend our old Baptist church on Sundays during our visits, there might be thirty people there instead of the crowds that would spill into the aisles when I was young. Rather than serving as an essential part of the nucleus that kept us together, church is now just a building where some people come to worship. It's no wonder that all the prisons are full.

To me, this change is not acceptable. All of us who care about that void need to do what we can to rebuild the village. Our youth need and deserve that. In eastern North Carolina, as in so many places where African Americans and other minorities often live in poverty, there is so much that could be done. Among other goals, we can certainly do more to strive for EQUALITY:

E – Educate. We must do everything we can first of all to educate society on the facts about life in these communities, and then we must expand our efforts to ensure that kids have the best possible opportunities for quality education.

Q – Question. We need to question the continued existence of everything that looks, sounds and feels like inequality. Why does it still exist? What can we do about it? We need also to question what we don't understand about equality.

U – Understand. Even as we seek specific changes to address inequality, we must understand that not everyone sees the situation through the same lens. People are different. We need to approach them with respect when trying to make changes.

A – Attitude. Our attitude toward equality usually defines how we think, how we act and who we are. It's important to examine our own attitudes and be honest about where we need to change them.

L – Leadership. We can all be leaders on the mission to attain real equality, and we do that by how we teach, preach and practice equality in our own thoughts and actions.

I – Integrity. We must always do what is right as it relates to inequality and our quest for true equality in life around us.

T – Trust. We must trust those that we educate, train, lead and mentor to exercise the virtue of equality and never compromise that value.

Y – Youth. Our youth are our future. If we don't educate and train them, who will? As we provide them the resources to improve their own lives, we must also instill the value of equality in these leaders of tomorrow because equality is a journey, not a destination. We must stay the course.

I remember one particular moment when I gained insight into the plight of many who live in that area I know so well. I was invited to speak to a Junior ROTC group at one of the high schools in eastern North Carolina, and I noticed one young man in the group who was acting in a rude and inappropriate way.

"What's up with that young man?" I asked the instructor.

"Well, I happen to know this young man's situation. He hasn't had anything to eat in a couple of days," the instructor explained. "His mother is the only adult figure in his life and he and several of his siblings are living with her on welfare, in the projects."

Moments like these tell me why I'm there, and fortunately I'm far from alone in my desire to make a difference in the lives of the young people back home. So many of my old friends and classmates have, like me, come back after achieving success in places far from home. They want to make a difference, too. I keep up with what's happening in my community even when I'm back in San Antonio through their updates, or through my contact with friends like Dr. Lonnie H. Blizzard, former president of Lenoir Community College. I never knew Dr. Blizzard until the fellow who mowed the lawn at my new second home told me about him. Then one day Dr. Blizzard knocked on my door, and a close friendship opened up.

He has his pulse on Kinston and surrounding areas, and he helps me to make sense of the big picture and envision how to change it.

It's not easy. I welcome the opportunity to individually mentor young people who have all but given up hope for their future, and although sometimes that's rewarding, sometimes it's challenging. Many young people today are quick to justify their discouragement. They point to their educational, economic and social hardships and say, "Life isn't fair." I nod my head but then I try to get them to think. "You're right, life isn't fair," I say. "The playing field is often not level. But if you work hard in school, at your job, in everything that you do, you can make a lot of progress in leveling that playing field. It will never be completely level, so what I would recommend to you is to play for the bad hops. Then, when they come, you don't let them hit you in the face and knock you out."

Sometimes I will tell them about my own story, not just my childhood but something that happened not many years after I left home. As you recall, I clung to a dream as a young boy of someday saving enough money to buy a house in Jones County so that I could finally own property. Well, when I was twenty-one and just back in the country from Vietnam, I actually bought a lot in Jones County. I had big-time hopes for the house I was going to build on that lot when I had the chance. While I was far from home, I believed that the taxes were being paid on the lot to keep things in line for my dream to be fulfilled. Unfortunately, the taxes were not paid. Ownership of that lot was taken away from me, and I was never told about what was happening until it was too late. I got a bad hop, and it broke my heart. From then on, I learned to play for those bad hops and to pay attention to details, in this case in the form of paying taxes and maintaining proper upkeep of any property that I owed. Bad hops like that one could come at any time, under any circumstance. Sometimes discrimination may be driving those bad hops, other times not. Either way, you've got to be prepared.

Some people I talk to have accepted poverty as their way of life. They work low-paying jobs, live in a rough environment and don't hold any visions of change for the future. They shrug their shoulders and try to explain that they just didn't have the same opportunities as others. I challenge them about that. I argue that opportunity, to a significant degree, is defined by the individual. "So, what opportunity did you afford yourself that would have made a better life?" I ask them. The reality is that we all control many of our opportunities. The system that we may have to deal with is just the system. We'll always have systems. We'll always have rules, regulations and policies. If you play to a side of the system that doesn't afford you the opportunity that you think you should have, you need to look at your own actions and beliefs. Keep looking for those ways in which you really can create your own opportunities, no matter what hand you are dealt.

While a few young or not so young people will resist the message, many others are hungry for this kind of direction. They just need many more individuals able and willing to deliver it to them.

One of the causes that I support back home is steered by the Jones County Community Development Corporation. We're trying to launch a community center to provide the young people in my home county a place to gather and engage in healthy activities, to stay out of trouble. We've got some roadblocks to plow through yet before this project really gets off the ground. At the same time, the organization has gone ahead with forming Movers and Shakers, whose goal it is to identify and honor 300 men (we need to include women, too!) who embody strong leadership and can mentor young people in need.

Awhile ago I was chosen to deliver the keynote address at an event that recognized the first fifty of these catalysts for change. I was honored to be among them and to have my story and achievements noted. As part of the ceremony, I was presented with The Order of the Long Leaf Pine, an award granted by the governor of North Carolina to individuals who have a proven record of extraordinary service to their communities and to the state. It was personally presented to me by a member of the family of our landlord when we lived and worked as sharecroppers on their land. I welcomed receiving the award from this man who, like me, was just a boy when we all lived within a system that fortunately dissolved.

I spoke to this group, as I often do, about the value of leading with Heart. I also touched upon the importance of all of us lending our hand as mentors. I noted that good mentorship requires a lot of time and energy, and that some people insist they don't have the time. Then I reminded them that we all have the same amount of time and urged them to find and use time for the young people of our county so that they can find their way to success and someday become good leaders and mentors themselves.

And that's what it's going to take to rebuild the village of caring, support and mentorship back in my home territory, and anywhere else in this great nation where young people struggle and the village has broken down or disappeared. We need to step up and do whatever we can to make a difference, and we must have faith that as more and more of us make this commitment, the young men and women of today will stand a better chance of fulfilling their own hopes for the future.

More than fifty years ago, Martin Luther King, Jr. inspired millions when he said "I have a dream." Today, all who hope to contribute to greater success and fulfillment for those struggling with hardships can build on a new DREAM:

D – Dedication. We must all remain dedicated to making a difference wherever and whenever we can. One hungry or homeless child, elder or veteran is too many. We must stay focused on the actions aligned with this dream.

R – Respect. As we continue to try to make a difference in the lives of others, we must see the good in everyone and help others see the good in themselves.

E – Education. All who desire have earned the right to learn. We must continue to encourage and support those in need to reach out for more education and to utilize it to the utmost to move forward in their lives.

A – Attitude. We can help those who are struggling to see the truth that if they want to change their lives, it begins with changing their attitudes. We can help them reshape and redirect their attitude in a positive and constructive direction.

M – Mentoring. We must continue to learn how to become better mentors, not only for our youth but for each other, and for all who desire positive guidance in their lives.

So wherever you are on your life journey today, my hope for you is that you can build your own pathway to success and fulfillment, that you remain humble as you do so, and that you commit to giving back to others whenever you have the opportunity to do so. Our nation and our world need you!

Made in the USA
Coppell, TX
11 June 2020

27347626R00121